With good wishes
to the Friday
Morning Club.

Lloyd D Emery

ON THE FLIP SIDE

ON THE FLIP SIDE

with LLOYD DUNN

BILLBOARD PUBLICATIONS, Inc./NEW YORK

Library of Congress Cataloging in Publication Data
Dunn, Lloyd.
    On the flip side.
    1. Dunn, Lloyd. 2. Impresarios—Correspondence,
reminiscences, etc. 3. Phonorecords—Industry and
trade. I. Title.
ML429.D9A3   658'.91'789910924 [B] 74-22385
ISBN 0-8230-7587-7

First Printing, 1975

To Priscilla…
"Because you're you."

In the past twenty-two years I have been in the music business, as an officer of Capitol Records. The company was started by Glenn Wallichs, astute businessman, Buddy DeSylva, top producer at Paramount, and Johnny Mercer, a very successful lyricist and popular performer.

For me it was a fun business. I was in the creative end. I listened to music, talked to talented artists, went to Broadway shows, traveled around the world. And got paid for it!

Many's the time when I would stop for a moment and "thank whatever gods may be" for my good fortune. I'd meet someone in, let's say, the canned tunafish business . . . and wonder how he felt . . . getting up every morning, shaving, dressing, traveling to work — all for tunafish. Not even a sardine to break the monotony.

In one of these moments of meditation I recalled a job I had at the pit of the Depression. For my younger readers, may I state that this period is not to be confused with the Recession, a minor lull you may have experienced. The Great Depression of the thirties was a ghastly grabber. It tightened its icy arms around every young man's dreams of a bright future, and hung on. For years.

A good friend managed to get me a job at the Seamen's Bank for Savings, in downtown New York. The salary was low. But every employee luxuriated in a free lunch in their lovely rooftop restaurant overlooking the harbor . . . white tablecloths, gleaming silver, uniformed waitresses and plenty of good food. To me, who had been lunching standing up with my hat and coat on, at the Exchange Buffet — where one could keep body and soul together for fifteen cents — this midday meal became a sheer delight.

But the job wasn't. They started me at the bottom. I was seated at a desk piled high with some sort of deposit slips and instructed to sort them in numerical, or alphabetical, order; my memory of the activity is mercifully hazy.

Every time I had almost cleared the table, an attendant would dump another huge mound on my desk. The only thing my boss ever said was, "You'll pick up speed when you get used to it."

Actually, I got used to it in the first two minutes, and was slowing down as my mind wandered, to avoid inroads of madness. After one week, the Exchange Buffet didn't seem all that bad.

I turned to the chap at a nearby desk who was doing the same kind of work but had developed a zombie-like efficiency.

"How long have you been doing this?" I asked.

"Two years," he said.

I got up, stretched, walked into my boss' office. And quit.

Of course that was many years ago. Now such drudgery at banks is relegated to huge machines that whirl about, flash lights, and spew out assignments in seconds. It's a bit confusing for the depositor, but charming miniskirted girls glide about serving you and one is glad to conform.

In the years that followed, I became a mediocre commercial artist, wrote advertising copy, True Confessions, movie scripts. I also played the banjo. Ultimately I ran my own advertising agency in Los Angeles. Capitol Records was my big account. I joined them in 1950.

Capitol Records' personnel consisted of a group of individualists — musical people, salesmen, lawyers, financial folk, and such. Their jobs were different, but they all had one thing in common.

They *all* knew how to pick a hit song. This included the chap who replenished the toilet tissue late every evening. And *me*.

Now, I know that nobody knows how to pick hits. But *nobody*. I'll give you a few examples.

One of our musical people had selected a song for Nat Cole, entitled "The Greatest Inventor of Them All." Rising to the enthusiasm of his presentation, we all agreed it *had* to be a smash hit. Didn't the lyric line remind us that God was the "Greatest Inventor," having created man, woman, and love?

Didn't it have religion going for it? And sex? And the voice of the great Nat Cole, caressing the melody and lyric? What else is there?

So the "B Side" — sometimes called the "Flip Side" — was selected from a group of "shelf songs" Nat had recorded, which we knew didn't have a prayer for hit status. Flip sides were always selected that way to encourage the disc jockeys to concentrate airplay on just the "plug" side, thus supporting our promotional effort, which in this case was considerable.

Well, "The Inventor" never got off the ground, despite the combined efforts of our sales and merchandising force, and a close tie-in with the clergy.

8

Pressed for answers, our promotion men told us it was the fault of disc jockeys. The idiots kept playing the *B* Side, about that dumb broad in a painting, *Mona Lisa*. "Every time they played it the switchboard lit up like a Christmas tree." Listeners liked it? They loved it!

"Mona Lisa" was Nat's biggest hit, and is still selling, years later, as I write these words. Nobody knew it had tremendous appeal except maybe the composers, Jay Livingston and Ray Evans. A song about a dame in a mouldy old painting, with a crooked smile? Jay — you've got to be kidding! Jay Livingston must have smiled, too, remembering another of his songs Capitol had previously rejected . . . "To Each His Own."

Such stories are endless, in all record companies. Especially successful ones like Capitol. For at that time, I recall that we had four of the top five hits on the best seller list, all by girl singers . . . Jo Stafford, Peggy Lee, Margaret Whiting, and Kay Starr. So we guessed right at least part of the time.

Yet we still talk of that recording session with Pee Wee Hunt, a popular trombonist whose orchestra played pleasant "two-beat" music with a Dixieland flavor. The musicians' union permitted the recording of only four songs in a three-hour period. Pee Wee had finished three, and there were just a few minutes left in the allotted time period.

"Play something —anything — quick!" our producer in the booth shouted, with an eye toward getting Capitol's money's worth.

And Pee Wee lit into "12th Street Rag," an old "standard," the same arrangement that had been played and recorded through the years. It sounded good. It always does.

"12th Street" became the flip side, to back up Pee Wee's next potential hit, which never happened. Because "12th St." took off like a rocket — straight up the sales chart.

But hadn't everybody heard it many times before? Sure! That's why they liked it. That's why they bought it. It's so easy to explain a hit after it happens.

Here's another story that bears repeating because it literally *shook the world*.

In 1955, Capitol was sold to a record company, headquartered in London — EMI, standing ungrammatically for Electric and Musical Industries. It was a huge outfit with over a half-century of success and a fine group of top executives. Their records were recorded and released everywhere in the world.

I was a V.P. in charge of Merchandising and Sales at that time. I remember, so well, a call from London. It was from Len Wood, a senior EMI executive who got in the act only when the international gears weren't meshing properly. The conversation went like this:

"Lloyd — how are you, old chap? I'm calling on a rather sticky problem. We have a record here we really *must* release in the States.

And your lads in A & R refuse to accept it. Frightfully embarrassing you know. Because the group is really . . . well, I must say . . . you know, they're selling here in a most gratifying fashion!" (That's British for "like hot cakes.")

I promised complete cooperation if for no other reason than that we had, occasionally, to ask them for similar favors. Despite the fact that EMI owned Capitol, all their companies throughout the world operate independently, and are responsible for their own sales and profits.

Besides, Len was a nice guy. We must help him out.

I called our man in "A & R," who selected artists and songs from affiliated companies, and prepared release schedules. Again, I quote:

"Lloyd, sure I know that thing. No, I didn't bury it. I played it, Lloyd, I played it. Lloyd, that kind of stuff went out of style in the early fifties."

He wanted to play it for me, but I told him to put it on release and quit arguing. I find that it's a mistake to listen to such records because my judgment is even more fallible. I like Dixieland and "pretty music," and they seldom reach the "top ten."

So the record came out. *And almost immediately the country shuddered and began to change.* Certainly never in history has anything musical had such an impact on man!

Oh yes . . . the song. It had a silly title. "I Wanna Hold Your Hand." Still sillier was the name of the group — The Beatles.

Capitol's manufacturing plants, strategically located, started pressing the record. They went on three shifts, and even then couldn't keep up. It was the biggest record the company — perhaps any company in the world — had ever released.

I then learned that Alan Livingston, Capitol's president, had received similar calls from Brian Epstein, the Beatle's manager, urging our support. A little local research unearthed for Alan these discouraging and amazing facts about previous Beatle records released in this country:

—A small company, V. J. Records, had issued several Beatles records . . . all "dogs." Sales were under 500 each.

— Swan Records, a successful little company in Philadelphia, then picked up the Beatles, releasing two records. They sold less than 1000 each. Swan dropped them.

To approve releasing more Beatle records, on Capitol — and promoting them the way Epstein insisted — Alan would have to be nuts. He was.

What's the answer? Who knows? Timing. Times. The Tune. And some strange magic that suddenly welds that vast army of volatile teenagers into one mass, chanting a new song. Because they like it. And perhaps, because their parents don't.

10

The chap who had rejected the Beatle record was *not* an idiot, I assure you. He had brought the company many of its top artists and biggest hit songs. I was with him one time in Paris, when he heard a happy tune being *whistled* by an orchestra, with just soft rhythm. The leader identified it for us, in almost unintelligible English, "No name, no name . . . there's no published music for it. For name we say 'The Poor People of Paris'."

He recorded it with Les Baxter and Capitol had another smash hit.

Lots of people have tried to develop formulas for hit records. They never work, of course. I have tried several "pretesting" methods — one of which involved getting a large, mixed audience together and measuring their emotional response to records, with some sort of electronic device strapped to their palms. Sweet, soft melodies showed little reaction. But when they heard Stan Kenton's blasting brass, they fell off their chairs.

What did this prove? Nothing.

One time a UCLA student came to me with a voluminous report he had developed for his thesis at graduate school. He had analyzed hundreds of hit records, over a decade. All these records had one thing in common — *and he had discovered it*. A gold mine!

I took the report and flipped through it to the last few pages. There it was . . . the magic ingredient. LOVE.

True, of course. Any idiot knows it. Love songs comprise the bulk of our catalog, whether called simply "I Love You," "I've Grown Accustomed to Her Face" — or "I Wanna Hold Your Hand." A better subject song writers can't find. I hope they never will.

But hit songs don't always involve lyrics about love . . . or about anything. I remember one that came from Toshiba, our partner in the Orient. Ku Sakamoto sang it in Japanese. It was called "Lonely Fool" and the lyric line, as explained to me, concerned a boy who loved a girl. But she was two-timing him . . . with other boys. So he left her, in a stormy parting. And now he walks alone, in the moonlight . . . looking up at the stars . . . so the tears will not run down his face. Lovely Japanese imagery.

Nobody could figure out Ku's Japanese words, but the tune *was* catchy. A Japanese word everybody knew was "Sukiyaki," so that title was slapped on the label. Three weeks later it was the Number One record in the country.

The executives at Toshiba were gratified but puzzled. Why the title? It was the equivalent of taking a song like "Love is a Many Splendored Thing" and calling it "Corned Beef and Cabbage."

I was V.P., International, then, and it was my job to explain it to my friends at Toshiba. As courteous people, they listened politely. But they didn't understand my explanation. Neither did I.

2

We had been sold down the Thames! A bunch of Limeys were going to tell *us* how to run a record business in *our* country!

EMI, headquartered in London, had bought Capitol Records! Those of us, and our staffs, who ran Capitol, went into an immediate state of shock.

Glenn Wallichs, our president, did his best to sell us. Among other things, EMI was the largest record company in the world, with top organizations everywhere. Including Red China! It seems that Chou En-lai, when a very young man, worked for the EMI company in Paris — Pathé Marconi. Perhaps as a nostalgic gesture, the EMI facility in Peking was not expropriated along with everything else during the revolution, but continued to operate in an isolated fashion. Every year EMI received a statement from China, and every year it showed an even break, with no profit or loss.

As we awaited the arrival of our new English owners, the atmosphere became charged with uncertainty and suspicion. "Don't fire until you see the whites of their eyes," was the watchword. News about EMI was "Paul Revered" around the office, with increasing anxiety. There was talk about having to change our coffee breaks to "tea tipples." We began to refer to each other as "old chap" and I answered the phone with "Dunn here."

When the first executive from London arrived to "look us over," it was my assignment to take him to dinner. I planned first to expose him to my wife and children, hoping to arouse compassion should I be destined for the block. Before I left for work, I lectured my wife, Priscilla, on her every move, particularly about being on time and not poking out her head from the bathroom, in curlers, while making her classic comment, "I didn't know it was so late." I was especially

13

specific about controlling our three young boys, ages four, six, and ten. They regarded soap and water with open suspicion, dressed sloppily, and lacked all the good manners that English children reportedly possess.

The next day I was introduced to a tall, slim, and dignified gentleman at the office, who seemed friendly enough. His name was Richard Dawes, and he had apparently been sent by EMI to reconnoiter before the big push.

That evening as I entered our driveway, I managed to carelessly touch the horn, to get everyone inside lined up at attention. I was moderately hopeful, but surely not prepared for the sight that was revealed when I opened the door.

There was Priscilla, exquisitely groomed, looking lovelier than I had seen her since our wedding. Beside her, standing erect, were Jeff, Steve, and Jon, wearing suits, shirts, and — hard to believe — neckties! I recognized the ties as mine, and was aware that their length necessitated tucking the ends in pants tops. But their coats were buttoned and the general effect was a visual delight.

As each boy was introduced, he stepped forward manfully and thrust out his arm for a formal handshake. Their expressions were grim, but most impressive . . . particularly when Priscilla later told me the whole show only required three hours rehearsal!

Then Dick Dawes — bless his memory — hugged the boys, picked up Jon, the youngest, carried him in his arms to an easy chair, and in no time had them all acting like normal American boys. We all warmed to the occasion and spent a delightful evening together.

The next day I took the light out of the belfrey tower and sent word around the office to put away the muskets and get back to tending the crops. All was well.

Then came EMI's Charlie Thomas, who taught my boys in pantomime how the English ride bicycles, while he brandished a martini. Many others followed. And I followed them. To England and around the world. It was by far the most challenging and happiest period of my business life.

* * *

Of all the successful — and difficult — stars in Capitol's galaxy, one name comes immediately to mind. To use a recording cliché, "Let's take it from the top."

Our sales staff, 350 strong, was having its annual meeting, at which time we presented new artists and recordings, along with merchandising programs. I was sales V.P. then, and tried to have such annual gatherings at places that were glamorous, to give the boys a chance to relax and think well of the management group.

We selected Estes Park, high in the Rockies. I felt that the men would enjoy the scenery, and get to bed early, there being little in the line of feminine companionship readily available.

One cannot, however, bat 1,000. That evening I noticed a Branch Manager seated at a cozy table with a charming girl he had apparently located among the tourists at the hotel. He was talking intently, with that same expression I have seen on his face when he was trying to unload overstock on a record dealer. My associate and I moved in closer, ultimately lurking behind potted palms right next to the table — like an old movie routine. This dialogue ensued — s'help me! The girl spoke first.

"Are you married?"

"I wouldn't lie to you. The answer is yes."

"Hmm . . . m . . . m . . . . What would your wife say if she knew you were asking me to go up to your room?"

Silence. Then . . . .

"We won't tell her."

Our guffaws put an end to the romance.

* * *

The day our first meeting was held, Alan Livingston, V.P. of Artists and Repertoire at that time, was presenting the new recordings, which were enthusiastically received by the sales people — who knew what was expected of them. Then came a pause in the presentation. Alan stood alone on the stage and spoke.

"Fellows, I want to tell you about a new artist we have just signed. He's not actually new, because a few years back he was a teenage idol. Then as all such stars must fade, he grew up and lost his audience.

"But he has tremendous talent. The kind of talent you *can't keep down*. So I signed him, and he is going to record for us."

Alan paused. Then he spoke the name.

"Frank Sinatra."

You won't believe this, but there was an audible *groan* from the group. I was in the audience, and heard the comments explode around me.

"He's got to be kidding!"

"Sinatra? Mitch Miller dumped him at Columbia. He's had it!"

"He couldn't get a job singing on the Jersey Turnpike!"

"God help us when we tell this to the dealers!"

The sentiment was echoed loud and clear — and painful. Frankie was great when the little girls screamed at him. And when he wore those white tails and sang "Old Man River" for MGM. But this is *today*. How come you dug *him* up, Alan?

Alan couldn't explain. How can you describe a voice . . . a magnetism . . . a sense of timing and phrasing . . . that makes old songs sound new, and new songs, as if they were sung just for you?

Among other things, I was in charge of album covers then. We asked Frank to come up to our photo studio for a cover shot or two. He had obtained an acting role in "From Here to Eternity" (no *singing*?). This kept him at the studio all day, so we had to work in the early evening.

He slouched into the studio, dog tired, but eager to please.

"What do you want me to do?" he asked.

A good question. He had started recording but no album concept had yet been set. I knew we had to grab the pictures while we could and work them into a cover idea later.

Those were the days when Frank Sinatra took direction, even from *me*. I faced him away from the camera, and muttered to Ken Veeder, our photographer, "Be ready to grab this — fast." Then I gave Frank this routine.

"You're walking down the street, going no place in particular. Suddenly a girl comes around the corner and passes you. She is *absolutely gorgeous*. What a figure! What eyes! What . . . but she's walking away, out of your life! Look over your shoulder at her! Quick!"

Frank looked. Ken snapped.

When I saw the print, I stared at it for a long time. Never had I seen such an expression of sheer delight, lust, admiration, desire — you name it — all wrapped up into *one glance*. (I kind of wished I'd seen that girl myself.) What an actor!

That was years ago. But the photograph is still used at Capitol, over and over. When you see it, remember this story. And while you're looking, see if there's a copy of his album "Only for the Lonely." We set up a prop lamppost, with a baby spotlight simulating the yellowed light. He slumped against the post. His expression, the angle of his battered hat, even the way he held his cigarette, made him the loneliest guy in town.

Sinatra's renaissance is too well known to need recounting here. A few years later it was my misfortune to be head of Artists & Repertoire when he decided to start his own record company with Dean Martin, a Capitol artist, and Sammy Davis, Jr. The fact that his contract with us still had a few years to run, bothered him not even slightly. He just told us.

We refused to release him, of course. He was a valuable asset to our company.

So he just stopped singing. For us, or anybody.

What can you do? Sue him, to *make* him sing, as per contract? Our lawyers said he couldn't record for anybody else, so we decided to wait it out.

We waited. And he waited. Month after month, the sad silence continued, broken only by our lawyers talking to his lawyers.

Ultimately we made a compromise agreement, wherein he made a few records for us, and some for his own label, Reprise. I still recall the episode with some bitterness.

But when I hear the guy sing now, on recordings with other labels, he still grabs me. It's a funny thing about Sinatra. There are probably a lot of people — important people — who have reason to dislike him. . . . But I have never run into one of them who didn't engage in "name dropping" occasionally.

"I was talking to Frank a while back. . . ."

"I remember, Frank used to say to me. . . ."

A great talent. A fine actor. I remember one time when Frank invited me to lunch at the Goldwyn Studios. . . .

* * *

If you've been in Hollywood, you may recall seeing, on Vine Street, a large building, absolutely round. There's a high collar around the roof, supporting illuminated letters reading CAPITOL RECORDS. And atop all this is a large "spike" with a flashing light at the peak.

Today, round buildings are more common. Holiday Inn, for example, has many. But at the time, in the mid-fifties, it was definitely kookie. Welton Beckett, a top architect, came in with the idea. After we saw his sketch, every building with sharp corners looked dull and routine. So we took a deep breath and said, "Let's build it!"

But now EMI owned Capitol! What would those staid English executives think of our plans? The only round building in all of Europe — maybe the world — was in Pisa. And you know what happened to that!

I could visualize EMI suggesting we change the plans to something a bit more conservative. Like a square structure with a flat roof on top and a polished brass plate on the door engraved "Capitol Records, Ltd."

No such thing! They loved the round building concept. And it wasn't long after we were digging foundations, pouring concrete, and looming up on the Hollywood horizon.

During the construction, we were the subject of much ridicule. So many wisecracks were made that I wrote a little booklet called "It's Been Said," containing all the witticisms collected to date. We gave it to local humorists, and suggested they get new material or refrain from comment. It put an end to tiresome repetitions of phrases like, "What speed does it turn at?" and, "How are you gonna chase your secretary into a corner?"

Sinatra gets my vote for the best *bon mot*. He stood in the center of one of our beautiful new recording studios in the finished building. It was perhaps the best and surely most modern in the world. Everything glistened, including the special flooring that floated on some sort of compound to insulate it from outside noises.

Frank looked slowly around. Then he removed the cigarette from his mouth, dropped it on the polished floor, and ground it in with his heel. "Somebody's gotta be the first," he said.

As the years went by and I watched musicians spilling drinks into our Steinways and tossing butts on the floor, I knew that the important thing was "Keep them happy." Our job was to maintain a climate where a lot of emotional and talented individuals could produce hit records. The phrase "Get it in the groove" explained everything. Pretty studios and fancy offices were fine. But Les Paul made the best of his early hits, recording in a beat-up old Hollywood bungalow, where he lived. He used the bathroom for an echo chamber!

* * *

Later, of course, came the Age of Efficiency Experts. By that time our company was sufficiently affluent to afford many departments on specialized nuances of management proficiency. One of these department heads retained an outside consulting organization to check over our inefficiencies. The chap assigned to Capitol was young and eager. No doubt, he was well qualified academically, and had recently completed a splendid analysis for perhaps the International Hazelnut Consortium, where his recommendations had resulted in firing all but one of the top brass — the chap who had hired *him*. So he knew how to "trim the fat" off our organization, to quote his own charming term.

From my point of view, the bulk of the blubber resided in the noncreative departments, which contributed nothing to hit recordings — which, incidentally, paid their salaries. But I had never been able to balance my own checking account, and was hesitant to get too articulate when such matters were on the docket for discussion.

Anyhow, this Efficiency chap ultimately appeared at my office door carrying an alarmingly big folder labeled *DUNN*.

Among our many inefficiencies was the booking of our three recording studios. Seems that they were empty until late in the afternoons, at which time the demand got so great that we had to rent outside studios at excessive costs. The remedy was quite obvious, and this chap had laid it out in a simple form that even an A & R man could understand.

We were to *schedule* our recording sessions in segments, with an hour between each one to allow for sweeping out cigarette butts, paper cups and other debris. The first period was 8:00 to 11:00 then 12:00 to 3:00, 5:00 to 8:00 and so on through the evening.

All this seemed reasonable — to the Expert. I hesitated to question his objectives, knowing I would be labeled noncooperative in his report to the directors. But that eight to eleven session in the morning . . . it bugged me. Musicians are notoriously late risers, and if forced to perform early their mood can be reflected in their music.

We finally approached Billy May, a great conductor-arranger with a sparkling sense of humor. He listened intently as the plan was presented. Sure, he wanted to help. Yes, he realized that such scheduling would make for greater efficiency.

18

But when we got to the early morning session for his orchestra, he stepped back with an expression of abject incredulity.

"My God," he gasped. "My boys don't start to throw up until noon!"

* * *

The Capitol Tower quickly became a major tourist attraction in Hollywood. Out-of-towners in fancy sportshirts poured into our lobby, slipped into studios, and rode the elevators. We finally decided to have organized tours — twice a week at 6:00 in the evening, when the offices were supposed to be empty. The tours started at the top floor, where lush executive offices were exhibited, and wound up in the recording studios below.

Many times, when I'd been working late, my door would pop open and strange eyes would stare at me.

"Who are *you*?" one brash woman asked.

"Stan Kenton," I replied. She seemed pleased.

I find that tourists seem to believe anything they are told, however implausible. For example, when friends or relatives visit us from the East, it has been my custom to take them around Beverly Hills, pointing out handsome homes where their favorite movie stars live. Actually, I haven't the slightest idea where movie stars live, but my guests always seem so thrilled that I feel I have done them a kindness, despite Priscilla's contention that the activity is immoral.

I point out to her what guides have told *us*, in many parts of the world. For example, at the Acropolis, high on the Parthenon (or maybe it was the other way around — I never could remember which was the hill and which was the temple). We were part of a tour group, sprawled on the steps in various stages of exhaustion, as the guide, radiating sincerity, talked.

It seems that Athena, in whose honor the temple was erected, was borne by her *father*, Zeus. Lacking the normal route of egress available to run-of-the-mill babies, Athena slithered about, finally emerging from her father's ear.

"It seems reasonable," I said to a friend, slouched beside me.

"It happens every day," he replied.

* * *

Hollywood's Chamber of Commerce was, of course, delighted to have our Tower and tours. Inspired perhaps by the tourist activity we generated, they decided to repave their sidewalks on Hollywood Boulevard and Vine Street, encompassing the names of great movie, television, and recording stars. Picking the names was tricky. I was one of a committee of five executives from the major record companies assigned to the job for our industry. We met weekly at the Brown Derby and argued.

19

Trying to recall big stars of past years was difficult. Such is fame. Kate Smith, of course. Paul Whiteman. And way back to my first recollection of a comedy record hit, "Cohen On the Telephone" (but *who* did it?).

At the same time, the movie groups were coming up with names like Francis X. Bushman and John Bunny. And, of all people, Mr. & Mrs. Sidney Drew (you'll find them on Vine Street!). Later it became apparent that tourists couldn't care less about old stars, to them unknown. And many current record stars came and went after only one hit record.

But we did our best. And finally the names and symbols in brass were inlaid in the polished pink cement. When the first rain came, the surface was like wet glass. I slipped into a backflip walking to lunch and limped on to the Derby muttering threats of legal action. Others I am sure, shared my experience. There is a tendency to lack enthusiasm for, let us say, Bing Crosby, when you've just banged your head on him.

I'm afraid it all didn't help Hollywood much. It's hard to define today just what Hollywood is. A tourist attraction it ain't.

But out of our meetings emerged the plan for organizing the National Academy of Recording Arts and Sciences. The idea popped up after a second round of drinks, and we all ran with it. Paul Weston of Columbia, Jim Conkling of Warner's, Bob Yorke of RCA, Jesse Kaye of MGM — and later, Sonny Burke of Decca.

Today, NARAS is a great success, with their national TV show, the Oscar-like award, called a "Grammy," and a huge membership. Meredith Willson won the first Grammy, and MC'd the TV show as The Music Man. It was all great fun, and still is.

* * *

At one point in Capitol's climb to success, our executives were required to take courses at the American Management Association, in their resplendent New York facilities. The paper work required kept me in a constant state of confusion, but I enjoyed some of the lectures.

I remember one talk given by a well-known psychologist, who has written several books about human relations in business. I shall call him Dr. Spiegelman. He was not an impressive man in appearance. But when he spoke, in a quiet, sincere voice, people listened. I liked what he said.

He told us that management courses were fine and helpful. Then he referred to AMA's basic definition: "Management is getting things done through *people*."

People. They were the vital ingredient. And no two were alike. They were all influenced by background, education, heredity and lots of other elements beyond the control of AMA.

I recall the bulk of his talk concerned the need for *consideration* . . . *sensitivity* . . . toward the people who report to you. All the rules and regulations — all the incentive systems and bonuses — are no substitute for the inspiration and guidance an executive can offer when he really knows the personality and aspirations of each person with whom he works.

I remembered a comment from another AMA lecturer: "You don't have to *like* a business associate to work well with him. An office is not a social club. Go ahead and do your job and forget about personalities."

Maybe so. But Dr. Spiegleman's comments made more sense to me. And when he finished his talk, the entire class of successful and adult executives gave him a standing ovation. Everyone felt he had contributed something important in this world of computerized formulas.

I was sufficiently inspired to visit Dr. Spiegleman after class and invite him to the Capitol Tower in Hollywood. Following the teachings of AMA, we had set up our own periodic lectures to "educate" perhaps three hundred of our second-string executives. Once a month they would gather in our largest studio to be "talked at." Most of the subjects were pedantic, and I felt empathy was sadly lacking. The good doctor would supply that priceless ingredient.

When the time came for Dr. Spiegleman's talk I got up and introduced him. I described his talk at AMA in New York and its effect on an audience of sophisticated executives. Everyone was ready to give full attention when he started to speak.

Dr. Spiegleman opened up with a joke. It could be typed as "A funny thing happened to me on the way to the Capitol Tower." It wasn't very funny.

As he went on he got even more jocular. Only nobody laughed, except a few polite, forced cackles.

But that didn't slow him up. This was Hollywood. Show Biz. Step aside, Shelley Berman!

It was a personal disaster, for me. Later, when he came up to my office, a big smile still on his face, I closed the door.

"Dr. Spiegleman," I said. "This is Hollywood. We make movies, records — our business is entertainment. Comedians we don't need. We've got them waiting outside our doors — good ones, with a natural gift to make people really laugh.

"What we don't have is people who can help us to be more understanding. Compassionate. Things like you told us at AMA. You didn't get one laugh there. All you got was gratitude and admiration."

His face flushed. "With your introduction they should have carried me in nailed to a cross," he said.

He departed later, with quiet dignity. I had a distant feeling I had mishandled the whole affair, and tried to get back to the job of making and selling records.

Today, of course, the subject of "sensitivity" has been honed to a lethal edge by endless universities and encounter groups. Even AMA had a whole course devoted to it, wherein a group of mature successful, executives were required to sit around a large table and lacerate each other's personal dignity. I was there. I remember one poor chap, a very prosperous printer from the middle west, being abused because he had "no sense of humor." From his reaction I cannot help but feel the man was emotionally injured by the incident, for he will be forever after trying to prove that he *does* have a sense of humor, which will change his charming, quiet personality — for the worse.

Somehow I feel the whole subject is getting too cerebral. Perhaps we should be looking into our hearts for the right answers.

3

It's easy to relax and have fun at your job when things are going well. And things were going very well at Capitol. We had been yapping at the heels of RCA and Columbia for a long time and now were beginning to pass them.

So everybody relaxed, and no doubt did a better job because of it. Among the top executives this was particularly true, perhaps encouraged by our president and founder, Glenn Wallichs, who enjoyed a bit of horseplay even more than his V.P.s did.

It was a tradition in the company to give jeweled pins for years of service. One year earned a little gold pin. Five — it had a ruby in it. Ten — two rubies. And so on up to 25, when I believe a minuscule diamond was imbedded in the pin. I always thought the idea was a bit corny and suggested that we give people something tangible for longer service, such as a picture of President Cleveland on a thousand dollar bill. But our personnel department assured us that these pins were treasured by the lower eschelon employees, and that they eagerly anticipated such luncheons with the presentation speech made by the officer in charge of the division. Maybe so.

In the line of duty, we were obliged to give such pins to our top officers. But somehow these presentations weren't coming off. Like the luncheon at the Brown Derby when Wallichs thrust my ten-year pin at me during the coffee, and said, "Here — I'm supposed to give you this."

"And you're also supposed to say something nice about me," I protested.

He hesitated. "I can't think of anything," he said.

I claim credit for originality in presenting pins to senior executives. My first effort involved the head of merchandising, Bud Fraser, who had survived ten years at Capitol — a two-ruby trinket. I'd have felt silly saying something nice about Bud. We knew each other too well.

So the night before the official luncheon in his honor, I froze his jeweled pin into an ice cube. Next morning I wrapped the cube heavily in foil and raced for the Brown Derby, presenting it to the bartender just as it was beginning to melt. I gave him careful instructions to put the cube in Fraser's drink.

We all arrived, and sat about lapping up our libations. I watched, fascinated, as Bud sipped his scotch and water. He didn't seem to notice anything strange. Perhaps the bartender had goofed.

Then he stopped drinking, a look of disgust on his face.

"There's a big fly in my ice cube," he said.

"That's silly," I said. "How could a fly get in an ice cube? Does it have two red eyes?"

"I don't know," he said. "And I don't care." And he flipped the cube out of the open door nearby.

It was a bit messy, finding the cube and restoring it to Fraser. I made him hold it in his hand while I eulogized his sterling qualities. All in all it was good fun.

* * *

Once a year, Capitol executives would go on a "road tour" around the country, presenting new artists and recordings to our sales staff, who would gather in five locations — San Francisco, Dallas, Atlanta, New York and Chicago. Each V.P. made an opening speech and we used to vie with each other to tell the funniest stories and get the biggest laughs ... thus proving to the boys in the field that we were regular fellows, with their interests at heart.

We opened at Pebble Beach once, and I told a story that was new at that time and brought down the house. The men roared with laughter, slapped each other on the back and repeated the payoff line. I remember making a mental note to institute a more generous bonus system ... a great group.

The story went like this ... and you can skip the next two paragraphs if you've heard it:

I started talking about a new research project we had just concluded concerning the characteristics of salesmen. I mentioned a few innocuous findings, then lowered my voice as I said how amazed I was to learn that ... and at this point I spoke so softly that my words could not be heard. My audience, intensely interested in view of my obvious concern, started shouting, "What? Say it again! Can't hear you!"

I raised my voice. "Most salesmen who are hard of hearing are homosexuals. What's the matter — can't you hear me?"

I guess it doesn't sound so funny in print — it's a sight and sound gag. But believe me, it worked at Pebble Beach. And when Glenn Wallichs followed me, he was pretty dull. Nice chap, but what can you do . . . .

When our little group moved on to Dallas, flushed with success and exuding confidence, I repeated my story. But here, my smash payoff line was received in the most grisly silence I have ever heard. I was embarrassed and annoyed, especially when later that evening most of the salesmen seemed to be trying to prove their heterosexuality by contacting charming girls in all the local bars, with complete disregard for the priorities of a V.P.

Only when we got home did I learn what had happened. Wallichs just couldn't keep from laughing his silly head off every time he saw me. He *had* to tell me how he had slipped back to the public address system while I was talking and turned up the sound level at the moment my voice dropped off, thus making the first mention of homosexuals seem like a genuine part of the report, and leaving a bunch of bewildered salesmen as I shouted the payoff line to their unasked questions.

* * *

Up went our business, and on went the gags. I remember, quite a while back, when TWA had sleeper planes from Los Angeles to New York. I was booked on one with Alan Livingston, who was a top executive at Capitol. Alan was one of those lean, handsome chaps who always exercised great personal discipline, never ate too much, and no fancy desserts. His drinking, too, was minimal, and he never leered at lovely stewardesses. It was maddening, because they frequently leered at him. Pudgy hedonist that I am, I found traveling with Alan limiting.

Alan arrived just before takeoff, having just been married to Betty Hutton. Both he and Betty had been involved in business commitments, so they had parted after the "I do's" and a gulp of champagne. That's Show Biz.

I knew about it, of course, and had planned an appropriate honeymoon for Alan. I ordered a lifesize, attractively colored photograph of Betty, in one of her most provocative poses. It was mounted on light plywood, cut out to follow all the appropriate curves, with the edges sanded round to avoid splinters.

I approached TWA well before the flight, requesting them to place the memento in Alan's bunk, with covers pulled up to the chin. They enthusiastically agreed to help. That's what I liked about TWA. Other airlines might not have taken a move without consulting the legal department and having Alan sign a release first, which would take a considerable edge off the gag . . . like 98%.

Alan arrived, calm and debonair, as he nibbled and sipped his way through a light supper and one cocktail. The whole staff and I were anxious to get him off to bed for the payoff. "Get a good rest, old man, and again congratulations," I said, heartily. He finally disappeared into the curtains of his bunk.

In a moment, he reappeared, chuckling, and grabbed me by the arm to take a look. I must admit, the effect was inspiring. In fact my only unhappy moment came when he failed to recognize my master touch and credited the whole thing to TWA.

But at the end of the trip, we were presented with a problem. What does one do with a lifesize model of one's bride? To jam it in the rubbish seemed ungallant. I urged that Alan take it with him to the hotel, but he, being the shy type, demurred. He also turned down as improper my offer to carry it.

Again, TWA to the rescue. Betty was given a position of honor in the Stewardesses' lounge where, for all I know, she still resides.

Alan is today married to the beautiful actress, Nancy Olson. After the ceremony, I saw them off on the plane. Nancy was real and lovely, but, sad to relate, sleeper planes had long disappeared.

* * *

Gags developed on planes are somewhat rare. But as it happens I do have another. It took place on a DC 6 from New York to Los Angeles. Joe Bushkin, a talented jazz pianist and Capitol artist, noticeably over-reinforced for the journey, staggered aboard just before take-off. Those planes, you may recall, had a circular lounge in the tail, which bounced and whipped about, but offered conviviality for travelers not susceptible to motion sickness. It was there Joe introduced me to Peter Donally, a noted raconteur who was at that time the M.C. of the radio show "Can You Top This." Talking about planes, stewardesses, and such, Peter told this story:

Seems that he and a friend once boarded a plane in New York for the night flight to Los Angeles. They added the customary two drinks to their already ample deposits, and became indignant when they learned that this was the legal limit while airborne on domestic flights. I suspect their protests became increasingly strident as they faced a long, parched flight. Anyhow, the stewardess finally "told them off," with ladylike dignity. Her position seemed to be that two people, notable in show business, should set an example of *good* behavior in public places, instead of being an annoyance and keeping the passengers awake.

Amazingly, the two were properly chastened and settled back in the lounge seats in a sulking silence broken only by the click-click of the stewardess' knitting needles.

After a period, Peter ventured a comment. What was she knitting? She told him it was a pair of sox for her boy friend. They were to be married very soon.

Peter meditated and grew increasingly sad. No lovely girl had ever knitted *him* a pair of sox. His melancholy mood developed to a point that the sox became a symbol of devotion. He wanted them.

So he told the girl he would buy the sox from her, naming a very substantial price. She was immediately intrigued, but said that she was only working on the first sock. She doubted if there would be time to finish them both.

Peter urged her to give it an old school try, stating that the handsome reward would be hers if she presented him with a pair of knitted sox when they touched down in L.A. It was up to her.

The young lady moved to a secluded far corner, and her needles clicked at a mad pace. The other girls, rising to the challenge, took over her duties and left her undisturbed. Perhaps the pilot slowed down the plane a bit — one never knows.

Anyhow, when the plane landed in L.A. she presented Peter with a box, gift-wrapped and containing the pair of sox she had knitted. He counted out the money into her soft palm, and they parted, exchanging wishes for health and happiness.

Peter said he didn't open the package until several days later. It contained two knitted sox, as agreed . . . one the normal size, the other a tiny duplicate that wouldn't fit a small midget. Instead of getting angry and screaming for a refund, he had them framed. He's that kind of a guy.

* * *

My friend Joe Bushkin, the piano wizard, was moved to tell a story, recounting a time when he played trumpet in an Army band during the war. He was due to blow taps at the grave of an elderly general. But the coffin was late in arriving and he passed the time sitting in the balcony of a nearby movie theater while consuming a pint of his favorite blend.

He managed to make the correct graveside area at the proper time, but midway through his performance, he swayed a bit and fell into the open grave. The colonel in charge was heard to state that it was only with the greatest difficulty that he withheld his order to fill up the hole immediately.

* * *

Back to the pin presentation. I knew my fifteen-year pin was due when Wallichs invited me for lunch at the Derby, and the other three V.P.'s appeared. So after a bit of business chit-chat I said, "O.K., Glenn — so let's have the pin. Get it over with."

He appeared puzzled, and brushed off the subject as he plunged into another business discourse. Lunch was over, and we left, with no presentation. Maybe he'd decided V.P.'s shouldn't get them. That was fine with me. I excused myself and headed for the nearby bank.

On the way back to the Capitol Tower, I passed the familiar boot-black stand, which was manned by a small unattractive chap of uncertain heritage. He shuffled forward and accosted me.

"Dis is fo you," he mumbled. And he gave me my pin.

* * *

A final word on such presentations. I knew that when Glenn Wallichs' next pin was due I would have to top all previous gags. So I planned a dinner, during which the entertainment would comprise a belly dancer, recruited from a Greek night club called "The Seven Veils." My plan was to have the girl wriggle up to Wallichs, pushing her body at him in pulsating enticement . . . gestures sure to irritate his wife Dorothy, thus adding to the fun.

The pin, of course, would be embedded in the dancer's navel. Glenn would be required to pry it loose while she twitched and made appropriate comments of endearment.

Alas . . . the best-laid plans. Poor Glenn became seriously ill, and was inactive for a long time following, in great pain from a rare type of bone cancer. His eventual death brought a sad ending to a happy and prosperous era.

During my early travels, I soon became aware that in Europe, and most of the world, American popular recordings were in great demand. It was in the mid-fifties and most of the foreign companies were recording in their own idioms — operettas and lieder in Germany, brass bands and folk music in England, chansons and such in France. And, of course, symphony orchestras and opera throughout the Continent, with strong provincialism influencing the selection of works, conductors, and soloists.

All as it should be. But the world had changed since the war, and young people with it. American music was new — exciting — vital. And they liked it. They didn't have the purchasing power of youth in the U.S.A., but they managed to scrape up enough shillings, francs, marks, and guilders to add up to a lot of money. And Capitol was at that time a leader in pop recordings.

"Those were the days, my friend." When I traveled abroad I was royally received and wined and dined in great style by the companies seeking Capitol recordings.

But our foreign associates insisted that we reciprocate by selling more of *their* records. They pointed out that there are more Italians in New York than in Rome. And more Germans in Milwaukee than — etc., etc. True, perhaps. But second-generation Europeans are *Americans*, particularly in their musical tastes.

But we tried. I worked with Dave Dexter, a highly creative recording man who was in charge of foreign releases. The two of us decided to develop a line of international recordings we would call "Capitol of the World." Album titles like "Honeymoon in Paris" and "Romance in Rome." (It may sound a bit tired today, but at that time it was a relatively new idea.) EMI had all these recordings, and it was simply a matter of presenting the idea to them and selecting songs. A pleasant way of making a living, we agreed, as we planned our trip.

It was a first trip to Europe for both of us. And a memorable one, in many ways. As there were no direct flights from Los Angeles at that time, we flew to New York, where we were booked on a TWA Constellation.

Several hours early, eager-beavers that we were, we arrived at the airport clutching our bags and trying to look casual and sophisticated. New York's airport, in the early fifties, comprised a scattered group of shacks that looked like temporary war structures, and probably were. If I expected a bit more attention and luxury from an airline than, let us say, on a flight to Hartford, I was disappointed. For we stood before the TWA counter in a crush of passengers, with no place to sit down. The room was overheated, crying children were underfoot — the place was a mess.

Our baggage was eventually checked in, and take-off time approached. But there was no announcement. We didn't dare leave the morass for fear of not being there at the golden moment of boarding.

Just as Dave and I were developing nervous twitches, there came a TWA announcement. There would be a slight delay in departure. No explanation accompanied the statement.

A moment later an announcement was made of Air France's departure for Paris. "Can't be any problem about weather," Dave said.

An hour more of surging and sweating and we were told the plane would be further delayed. In the interim, several other foreign carriers had taken blithely off with their happy passengers. I fumbled for my Rolaids, realizing that we had dates set up throughout Europe which now threatened to collapse.

Another two hours passed. After a bit of pushing and elbowing I faced the man who had been issuing the proclamations and asked him what was wrong.

When he deigned to reply, it was to the effect that there were *problems.* End of discussion.

By this time our group of passengers had become somewhat unified. I was asked, "Waddihisay?" Leadership was thrust at me, and I was expected to lead the rabble and storm the ramparts.

At that moment came the announcement of Pan Am's flight to London, leaving on time, at 8:00 P.M. I hastened over and discovered that the plane was not full and they would be happy to accept TWA passengers. In answer to a fresh batch of "waddihisays," I announced that Dave and I were switching to Pan Am. A cheer went up and most of them joined me. With a group of followers at my back, I approached the TWA desk to get our baggage and tickets back.

Here I encountered opposition. I was told that if I wanted to transfer, go ahead — and, personally, good riddance. But to incite a group of contented passengers into open rebellion was intolerable!

I assured him that I hadn't done any inciting. The group must have recognized my executive capacities, and looked to me for leadership.

Unmoved by my contentions, he continued to regard me as a troublemaker. Our voices rose above the crowd, and our confrontation became so close that I could read his TWA badge of authority. He was in charge of Public Relations. His Relations intensified when he came at me from behind the desk, threatening to do me bodily harm. In fact he clutched my necktie and pulled me up to him, nose to nose.

Let me freely admit at this point that while I may be a leader, I am not a fighter. I had engaged in fisticuffs only once in my life and the encounter left me beaten and bloody.

I remember it vividly. I was a new student in the seventh grade of P.S. 152. Family fortunes were failing and I had transferred to this public institution of learning from Adelphi Academy, a private school. I was therefore regarded by my peers as a coward and a sissy. Looking back, I am sure they were right.

Every school has its bully, and this one was more than amply endowed. Amazing that decades later I can still remember his name — Watson Booth.

It was in those pre-zipper days, and his ploy was to walk up beside me with an apparent air of comaraderie, then with a sudden sideways lunge he would rip open the fly of my pants. This act of aggression effectively removed all the buttons, making it essential for me to spend the afternoon session clutching my groin, which suggested to at least one teacher that I was engaged in extracurricular activities.

My fellow students, cruel and fiendish as many boys are at that age, loved the routine. It brightened up the lunch hour, and no doubt diverted the sadistic talents of Watson Booth away from them.

Child that I was, I knew that the time had come when I had to put up my dukes. One noon, anticipating his customary swipe toward my genitals, I counterattacked with a desperate blow that caught him on the chin.

According to my calculations, he should have been knocked flat on his back. But it was apparent that my first pugilistic effort had merely served to stimulate him. He stepped back, with an expression of sheer delight as he said, "So yuh wanna fight, do yuh?" I didn't, but I did. The crowd clustered around like Romans when the gates lifted to let in the lions.

In no time I was flat on my back with a nose spurting blood. I hadn't seen much of my own blood, and it was frightening. But under the urging of the crowd, I rose to fight again. And again I went down, with my head hitting the pavement — *hard*.

The crowd suddenly scattered. I was pulled up to my feet by a strong adult arm.

"Dunn," said the Voice of Authority, "I don't know what went on at Adelphi, but let me assure you that we don't tolerate that kind of bullying here!"

I couldn't answer. I was sobbing.

*   *   *

But I have digressed. Let me get back to the TWA counter where I stood, clutched by the Public Relations Man.

My colleague, Dave Dexter, was a sturdy chap with a notable record of athletic achievements. He stepped up to be of help, as I grew angry and began to push. The TWA man must have remembered his job description did not include the luxury of belting passengers, for he quickly dropped back, and apologized, grabbing my hand and pumping it. I assured him that there were no hard feelings and I would like to proceed with transferring the baggage to Pan Am.

I suppose there were about ten or twelve of us in the group that moved to Pan Am's luxurious Stratocruiser. We left promptly at eight, on time. And then follows the payoff — for TWA!

The Stratocruiser landed, not in London, but in *Boston* . . where we were delayed for *two whole days.* I mean *forty-eight hours* were devoted to repairing something essential to flight that was hourly reported on the verge of rectification. We were ensconced in the best hotel, permitted to dine in the finest restaurants of our choice, and see any show of our selection. Despite all this there was a noticeable coolness in the attitude of the former TWA passengers toward me.

Unkindest cut of all, I learned that TWA took off an hour after we did, and sailed smoothly to London without incident.

Today, with everything beautifully organized by airlines, backup planes available, Clipper and Ambassador Clubs ready to serve you in all major airports, courtesy and consideration at every hand, it seems hard to believe what we pioneers went through in the early fifties!

*   *   *

Sir Joseph Lockwood, head of the EMI empire, was particularly impressed with American marketing methods. I believe he was the one behind the plan for a merchandising forum, to be presented by Capitol's staff in Paris. All the EMI companies from throughout the world would attend, and listen while Capitol told them new, exciting methods of displaying, promoting, and selling records. It was a great opportunity for our underpriviledged colleagues, we felt.

It quickly became obvious that the audience did not share in our feelings. The general attitude was perhaps best expressed by a remark overheard by me in the men's room. "Vot dos Dunn tink he iss — a forking genius?"

Generally, there was polite acceptance of our offerings. But it was always qualified by the phrase "Our country is different."

And of course they were right. How could the United Kingdom promote pop records through disc jockeys when BBC, at that time, played such music only two hours daily, in the afternoon? Why should Vienna adopt self-service when they didn't have enough recordings to supply the customers who patiently waited in line at the record counters? And on it went. For it was in the middle fifties — pre-Beatle days, with the scars of war still healing.

For example, the recording studio, where we held our meetings, was owned by Pathé Marconi, our French affiliate. It was a wartime relic, I was told — insulated for soundproofing with quantities of straw held against the wall with chicken wire. Rats had nested throughout the straw, and eaten it away in spots.

One of our executives told me he had recorded a violin soloist there, right after the war, in mid-winter . . . with no heat available. The violinist wore his overcoat, a hat, and woolen gloves, cut off just above the knuckles. The accompanist? He sat on his hands, until the moment for each "take."

Attached to the studio was a small food counter, run by an attractive French girl, who spoke not a word of English. It was here that Fred Rice, our talented display artist, reached his finest form. For we had breakfast there each morning. And Fred sketched out on napkins exactly what each of us wanted.

So what? Try drawing two fried eggs — over easy. And two more, sunny-side up (with bacon, crisp!). The only mistake during our entire stay was Fred's version of a half of grapefruit. She thought it was an orange. But she didn't have either, so no problem.

Fred's drawings were treasured by the young lady, along with memories of his charm and wit . . . which was all very well during breakfast. But I remember one time when I got quite annoyed by his talent. It was late evening and a group of us had wandered into a bistro coyly called Le Sexy. Fred started to sketch one of the girls there and we were immediately surrounded by many others, waiting for their portraits. It was all very amusing until I got the bill and discovered I had to pay a substantial fee for each girl. Why, I asked? Because they had entertained us!

Our presentation was climaxed by a large and formal dinner party, given for the visiting executives and their wives by Pathé Marconi at a very plush establishment. How well I remember that evening!

We were staying at the huge and revered Grand Hotel, in Paris, near the famous Opera House. I don't know how old it is, but I can easily visualize Napoleon demanding a room from an indifferent desk clerk while Josephine lurked in the background. Some improvements have no doubt been made since then, but nothing to change its basic charm.

When we returned to the hotel early that evening, it was already dark, and barely time for a quick shower and getting dressed. We hurried across the lobby.

The first mistake was unquestionably mine, though perhaps understandable. For the various floors of the hotel are not numbered in traditional fashion, and we were left off on the wrong one. As all floors look alike, I quickly jammed my key into the lock. I twisted and tugged considerably before I realized that this room was not ours.

Then I removed the key. Or rather I tried to. It was firmly stuck in the battered lock and would not budge.

At that moment *all lights in the hotel went out*. Never have I seen such blackness. We stood, huddled together for a few moments, then groped our way down the hall to the elevator. It was not working, of course, having gone out with the lights.

Working our way down the curving, stygian staircase was an experience. There were others similarly occupied, and there were squeals and protests in several languages, as we descended it like mountain climbers, clinging together.

The desk in the lobby was illuminated by two flickering candles, with the clerk between them looking like a judge at the Inquisition. He responded to all frantic inquirers with a Gallic shrug, but when I explained my dilemma he affected genuine concern, falsely arousing my hopes. I must say he seemed grieved as he told me there was no other key to my room. No, *not one*. End of discussion.

What was I to do? I raised my arms and clasped my hands in the international gesture of entreaty. He shrugged his shoulders again and disappeared through a rear doorway, carrying one candle.

Attendance at the reception that night was imperative, for we were honored guests. We stumbled our way back upstairs, counting the landings, ultimately arriving at our floor. We knew it was ours because there were Bud and Kathy Fraser from Capitol, who roomed next door to us. Wonder of wonders, Bud was standing in illuminated glory, holding a fragment of candle aloft in a Statue-of-Liberty fashion.

Ever resourceful, he quickly comprehended our problem and disappeared into the blackness. He looked like Marley's ghost when we saw him returning down the hall, clutching the hand of a plump chambermaid. She had a huge ring of keys, from which she eventually extracted one that opened our door. We gratefully entered our cavern.

But of course we had not a glimmer of light. Here again Bud rose to the occasion. Taking a razor blade, with surgical skill he halved his two inches of candle — a neat trick considering that the candle was lit, for he needed the illumination to avoid cutting off his thumb.

The light was dazzling, and we were tearfully appreciative. However, the activity had interested two elderly ladies across the hall, who had been desperately trying to twist into girdles and gowns in pitch blackness, to attend the opera.

Fraser, ever the gentleman, halved his half of the candle, reducing each to about a half inch. He did have the advantage of my candlelight for this surgery, but it was neatly done, and we all departed to dress, with the ladies pledging friendship eternal and hoping we would visit them if we ever passed through Omaha.

Our descent down the staircase was triumphant, holding our two candles aloft and locked together for security — all handsomely gowned and groomed.

When we returned late that evening, the lights were on! We happily reached the correct room, but noted an elderly gentleman in overalls standing high on an old wooden stepladder, blocking our door. He was fumbling with some wires that ran along the moulding at the top of the hall, into some sort of fuse box. We stood patiently while he prodded.

Suddenly there was a shower of sparks and the lights again went out, followed by a great thump in the blackness, which proved to be the workman, who had fallen from his perch, with the ladder on top of him. This respite gave us the opportunity to enter our room, where we undressed in the darkness and fell gratefully on our beds.

Thinking back, I can't help but wonder what happened to the chap who found our key stuck in the lock of his room. The problems he faced in the blackness of that hotel boggle the mind!

* * *

I cannot leave Paris without mentioning its taxicabs . . . though I shudder at the very memory. For though the cabs vary in size and shape, the drivers are *uniformly difficult.*

I do not think I can remember getting into a cab in Paris when I didn't wind up in angry debate. Nothing was ever settled, perhaps because the drivers spoke no English and I no French. But basically, I believe it was due to their uncompromising attitude about where you were going, and your refusal to consider a much better place that they recommended.

It may be unfair of me, but I have often suspected that many Parisian cabbies enjoy a small kickback from certain establishments to which they can maneuver tourists. But even when honest mistakes are made, they are unyielding.

Like the time I jumped into a cab and clearly ennunciated "Hotel Rafael!" where I was staying. The trip seemed to take longer than normal, and when we reached our destination I found the Eiffel Tower looming above me. In French it's "Tour Eiffel," and I supposed my Brooklynese confused him. So I apologized, wrote out the hotel's name, and started to get back in the cab. But he would have none of it.

I explained that I had been to the Tour Eiffel several times, and since it was late in the evening, desired sleep. I would be happy to pay the additional cost of my stupidity. But he ejected me, and took off with another fare.

One time in Paris, Priscilla and I left our hotel in a cab, headed for the Dinazade, a superior restaurant where we were to meet friends for a dinner party. The driver took us to the Scheherazade, which, he assured us, was a much better establishment.

We told him we were meeting friends, but he refused to move on, and involved the Scheherazade doorman in efforts to shanghai us. Both men were angry, and I had a feeling that we were somehow at fault. Finally I demanded to be taken back to our hotel, for a face-to-face confrontation with our doorman. I had been told cabbies fear doormen perhaps because they control fares and destinations. It worked, because at that point the cabbie drove us to our proper destination. I gave him an extra tip, because he was quite upset about the whole affair.

* * *

Where night clubs and female companions are concerned, I am sure many such institutions reward cab drivers for their dedication. I was convinced of this one night in Pigalle. As some of you older boys may know, this area of Paris is devoted largely to "Girlie Shows" in varying stages of nudity. Normally I find such displays tedious, but I had gone there with Bob Myers, head of our classical recording. It was his first trip to Paris and he had wondered where all that sexy stuff he'd heard about went on. We had visited an establishment, and I had become annoyed when a flashy and fleshy showgirl had put her hand on my knee while her artificial eyelashes semaphored signals that set waiters popping champagne corks.

Anyhow, it was late and I was tired so I left Bob, who had become intrigued with a performance involving a young lady disrobing to the strains of Debussy. He said Debussy was so programmatic — whatever that means.

I wandered into the square where a number of cabs were clustered. When I stepped into the first one and named my hotel, he waved me out angrily. I approached another and was barred before I could open the door. Soon I realized that I faced a Maginot line of drivers, determined to stand against me.

I stood before the whole group, hands outstretched in entreaty, as I cried out the hotel's name with increasing poignancy. I sought only the solace of sleep. Why, oh why, was I rejected?

Then one man stepped from the group and addressed me in perfect English. He was tall, well groomed, and had a flowing mustache. He stated with angry emphasis that he was ashamed of his fellow drivers for their treatment of a guest in his country. He apologized for them. Such men gave the country a bad name. Because all they wanted was to take a fare to a place where entertainment and *girls* were available. They made a small commission on such deliveries. A trip to a hotel at that hour offered inadequate compensation. They preferred to wait around for a live one. Then he bowed graciously, opened the door of his cab, and said "*I* will take you to your hotel!"

I was deeply moved by his forthright speech and friendly attitude. Off we drove, into the night.

But we had barely gotten under way before he turned his head and said with a sly grin, "You would like to meet some lovely girls?"

I must confess, his remark jarred me. But I thanked him, stating that I was too old for such peccadilloes. I clutched at a wisp of my gray hair to dramatize the point.

A moment later he tried again. Perhaps I would like to watch a show. He wasn't too clear, but it seemed to include a cast of three sexes.

Again I declined, not daring to get angry, for fear of being abandoned on a strange dark street. But this time I placed my hand on his broad shoulder and addressed him thus: "Listen. I am a musician, a professional musician. Back in America I play at such establishments you have suggested we visit. I am here for a holiday. Surely you, for example, would not want to ride around in a cab on your vacation?"

"You — a *musician*?" he said. "I, too, am a musician!"

He played the trumpet. And he suggested that we stop at a small place, where we could have a beer together and talk about the music business.

I agreed for three reasons. First, it seemed the lesser of the evils thus far offered. Second, I was beginning to fear that further refusals would ultimately earn me a bash on the head followed by a sojourn in some dark alley. And third, I was intrigued by the prospect of conversation with such a colorful character, surely resulting in a story or two to tell the folks back home.

We drove through several dimly lit streets and stopped before an unmarked door, illuminated by one bare light bulb, and surrounded by rubbish cans and litter.

I looked at him, uneasily. "It's the back door," he said reassuringly.

And it was — the back door to a glittering clip joint with a stage show of writhing bodies. Before my eyeballs adjusted to the low-key lighting, I was thrust into a chair, bracketed by two girls, two waiters popped two champagne corks while glasses were thrust before us. The cab driver had disappeared.

I jumped from my chair and headed for the door, but I was stopped by a large, muscular chap and escorted back to my table, where I was presented with a check.

It cost me almost fifty dollars to buy my way out, which was about ten dollars a minute for my stay. I paid it, coward that I am, and stepped into the street.

My cab driver was there, smiling affably. "Get in," he said, "I'll take you to your hotel without charge."

I did, and he did, proving he wasn't all bad. And his limited conversation on the way concerned a recommendation regarding my future activities. "Don't try to beat the system."

* * *

Many tourists are familiar with a club in Paris called "The Crazy Horse." I've been told it's owned and operated by Americans. Perhaps so. Anyhow, the entrance looks like something at the top of a subway station. When you descend the stairs, you find yourself in a smallish room packed beyond capacity with overheated bodies.

This overheating is caused not only by the normal BTU's humans exude, but with the temperature rising as the floor show progresses. To call it a "strip joint" would be like referring to Beethoven's "Moonlight Sonata" as a "tune." For here disrobing is done with consummate artistry by truly beautiful young women. Each episode follows a story line, and while the plot is elementary it does represent civilized inroads into the old tasseled and tasteless routines.

I was there one night with Priscilla, trying to show her the spice of Paris without the sordid side. John Coveney, head of our classical artists' relations, had joined us, and the three of us were locked together against a table about the size of a coffee can top — the one-pound size. We clutched our drinks in alarm as additional people were pushed into areas made available when one exhaled. There was enough air to sustain life, I suppose, but I am sure the kind of canaries they used to test the air in mines would not have survived.

The room grew quiet as the lights dropped and the curtain rose on the small stage. The first act concerned a young schoolgirl, evidently of college age. Exceedingly lovely she was, yet interested in her studies with a most commendable dedication. For as she reclined on the bed in her small dormitory room, and oh-so-slowly undressed, she kept reading some text book . . . a philosophical treatise, as I recall, quite erudite for one of her age.

The room was now completely silent, accented only by gasps of breathing as the audience struggled against suffocation, and perhaps passion. Her outside garments had been removed. And as we were getting down to more intimate revelations, the lights kept dimming, following the Crazy Horse tradition, or perhaps a legal requirement.

Still dimmer grew the lights. And more exposed the lovely lady. But she kept reading, occasionally flicking a page as she progressed.

And then I heard John Coveney's voice. He spoke softly, but his voice echoed through the quiet room.

"She'll *ruin* her eyes," he said.

It brought down the house. And the curtain with it, shortly thereafter. For sex and humor are seldom compatible.

As an added fillip, when the lights came up, Priscilla clutched my arm and gestured toward two people directly in front of us, now rising to leave.

"Who are they?" I asked.

"Idiot," she hissed, "it's Princess Grace and her husband from Monaco!"

And so it was. I remember, because she once recorded for Capitol a duet with Bing Crosby. It was Cole Porter's "True Love," and it won her a record industry award. A lovely song.

* * *

Perhaps to prove that Paris is not all bad (how could it be, set in such beauty?), I'll relate a pleasant memory from my first visit. Bobby Weiss was "our man in Europe," single, sophisticated and astute. When he arrived at the hotel to take me and an associate to dinner, he was accompanied by one of the most beautiful girls I have ever seen. Her natural beauty was enhanced by a high fashion gown, hat, gloves — the whole bit.

We stepped away from the hotel and reached a crosswalk. As we were about to enter it, a small car drove up and jammed on the brakes, blocking our passage. The car had an opening at the top and through it popped the body of a man who looked at us, waved his arms, and poured out a torrent of French phrases. Then he dropped back into the car and gunned it away.

"What the hell was his problem?" I asked Bobby.

"Nothing," Bobby said. "He was just commenting on my girl friend. He said her beauty was a joy to behold. And her dress — magnificent!"

Ah Paris! Where else could such an incident occur?

* * *

Come to think of it, there was a similar incident I recall, in America. I had just met Fumiko Suga at the Los Angeles airport. She was the lovely daughter of the president of our affiliated company in Japan. She had come to visit America, and stay at our home.

We stopped for lunch at "The Warehouse," a restaurant on the water at Marina del Rey. Fumi was sitting there, big black eyes shining, when a young man stopped at our table and said a few words to her in halting Japanese.

She seemed embarrassed when I asked her what he had said. When I pressed her, she spoke shyly, "He said I was very . . . beautiful."

I rather liked his effrontery. But I suspect if I did the same thing in Japan, some irate escort would reward my gallantry with a judo chop.

* * *

More about Paris. This time with Bill Mikels, a colleague from Capitol. Bill had never been there. He said he was near France once, but his ship was torpedoed in the Mediterranean and he wound up living with some Arabs, until the Army located him and assigned him to a remote part of China, engaged in some sort of radio espionage. A run-of-the-mill Army experience, I gathered. So he was pretty excited as he settled down in first class on TWA's direct flight to Paris, anticipating all the goodies ahead.

We had reached our altitude and I heard his voice, *"They've got to be kidding!"*

Immediately thereafter I heard a high-pitched, cracked voice say, "May I get you gentlemen something to drink?" She was a sweet and gracious lady, somewhat older than the average stewardess — by about fifty years. Seems like she was one of TWA's *first* stewardesses. She therefore, I suspect, had seniority, and could choose any flight she desired . . . obviously selecting Paris over, for example, Pittsburgh.

There were other businessmen in nearby seats, and after the shock of initial impact we got rather fond of her and were glad that the union, or somebody, had protected her job. Any flight can be dazzling with gorgeous creatures serving you, but Senior Citizen hostesses are unique.

"Mother, another of your home-cooked martinis," Bill would say, and she'd serve it in a shaky, spilly fashion but with a warm maternal smile. There were two other hostesses helping her, but we gave Mother the big rush and she seemed to thrive on it.

It was early evening when Bill and I got to Paris. I like to stay at the Lancaster, which is small, elegant, and just twenty steps from the Champs Elysées, where all the action is. After checking in, we strolled around stopping for a cocktail or two at Los Calvados, a plush restaurant nearby. And here happened an amazing incident.

As we entered the lounge, a voice greeted me. I recognized George Jessel, well-known theatrical personality. I had met him once or twice through Glenn Wallichs, and I suppose he remembered my face, though surely not my name. I introduced Bill, who was impressed with my jet-set connections.

Jessel insisted we join him. He ordered drinks for us, and of all things, a sandwich for himself . . . a strange selection for the place and the hour. His conversation was limited and vague, and he seemed intent on consuming the sandwich rapidly.

Then he asked for the check. When it came, he discovered that he had left his wallet in his hotel room.

40

I took the check, assuring him that it was something that could happen to any of us. I remember the occasion well. The amount was around twelve dollars, and I gave the waiter a twenty. The waiter reappeared with a tray containing my change, in francs.

I will now relate an incident that you may not believe but s'help me it happened — as Bill Mikels will verify.

Mr. Jessel leaped to his feet, scooped up my change, and dashed through the door into the night.

"That was *your* change!" the waiter exclaimed.

"Yeah — what happened?" Bill added.

I don't know. I haven't figured it out to this day. But I did tell Glenn Wallichs I was putting it on my expense account. After all, Jessel was *his* friend.

* * *

All this reminds me of the time I left Paris on an early flight for London. I was reclining in an aisle seat, yawning, when the stewardess offered me champagne. It was shortly after 9:00 A.M., so I rejected it in favor of black coffee.

Then I noted with surprise a familiar face, across the aisle, one seat forward. It was Norman Tyre, a prominent lawyer from Hollywood, who represents many famous motion picture and recording stars.

I leaned out in the aisle, slightly forward, and said in a stern voice, "Anyone who drinks champagne at nine in the morning is a *lush*!"

Now I have seldom regarded lawyers as being endowed with too much in the line of humor. But his rejoinder was immediate. Without looking back — without knowing who had made the remark — came his retort.

"Anyone who turns down free French champagne is an idiot!"

Touché! I joined him in a glass of the bubbly.

5

"Show it like it is, man!" shouts today's photographer, as he throws sidelighting on a young artist's face to play up his pimples for an album cover.

Yeah, yeah — I know. Today things are for real. No pink lights. No phony palm trees. And *never* any retouching!

My son Jon has a whole pile of albums with such covers. "How do you tell the boys from the girls?" I asked him. Same long hair. Same dirty dungarees. Same shapeless shirts.

Then I realized. Of course . . . the boys have beards.

Well, fellas, I can tell you it was different in my time. When we got hold of a girl (for an album cover), our finished photo would set you to dreaming dreams. Even fat opera stars came out slim and sexy. It was an art. And it was fun.

And it sold a helluva lot of albums.

My career in album covers started when my advertising agency acquired Capitol as the big account. In addition to ads and such, we did their covers and wrote the pitch on the back.

I remember . . . came that wonderful development, 33-1/3 RPM. Capitol issued a flood of ten-inch LPs in leatherette paper jackets, stamped with the album title and artist's name. The whole industry was following the same style. But ours had a bit more class. Pops were blue with silver type. Classics, maroon and gold.

We started talking to Capitol about *illustrated* covers, using photos in full color. "But how can you picture a product you can only hear?" they asked. I showed them a current ad, still used, showing a violin virtuoso holding aloft his fiddle, while his other arm embraces his accompanist, irresistible in her new perfume. You could only *smell* that product. But it was the scent of romance for lots of girls who bought it.

Then Capitol recorded a new album featuring eerie quaverings of the electronic Theremin. They wanted to call it "Music Out of the Moon." The artist and instrument were relatively unknown.

Stamp that exotic title in plain type? So it looks like every other album on the record rack? Never!

Photographer Paul Garrison, art director Jerry Navoor, and Lloyd Dunn came up with a better idea. An actual photo — in glorious color — of a gorgeous moon maiden stretched out on an exotic lunar landscape! (This was before the rocket ships ruined our illusions.) She was scantily attired for those days. Capitol was a bit jolted, and made us retouch out the young lady's belly button. "Maybe they don't have them on the moon!" I told our disgruntled art director.

They tell me the album made history — piling up endless sales from lots of people lured to listen by the cover. Capitol quickly followed with more Theremin — an album called "Peace of Mind."

Not wanting to upset a successful formula, we decided to show a provocative young girl in the near-nude, spread out on a cloud, dreaming peacefully. I decided to personally supervise the photo session, as any dedicated account executive would.

We got to the studio early, set the lights, and waited. The model came through the door, glowing with youthful loveliness.

Closely behind her was a plump, middle-aged woman. Her mother.

And a real spoil-sport Mother was, cramping our creativity by insisting on personally arranging the fine spun-glass we were using to produce a cloud effect, and cover the strategic areas on the model.

The photo came out fine. But the spun-glass particles didn't. Thousands of tiny glass particles remained stuck in the young lady's satin skin and couldn't be brushed out.

I guess it's pretty uncomfortable when you find yourself with endless glass particles stuck in your strategic areas. Her mother retained a lawyer to discuss the problem in depth with Capitol's legal department. My offer to personally pluck out each fragment was not considered amusing.

* * *

I could go on. But I wanted to give you some idea of the problems we pioneers faced as an endless stream of illustrated album covers followed. Background music was particularly susceptible to pictorial interpretation. We started with "Music for Romancing." To save money we used Capitol's youthful V.P., Alan Livingston, as one model. The other was my wife, who still complains because I showed only the back of her head. I guess such albums don't sell well today. I remember my last title suggestion, "Music for Magic Moments in Motels," was rudely rejected.

Covers, of course, got fancier and more expensive as competition picked up the challenge. I recall Jackie Gleason insisting on retaining Salvador Dali for his new album "Lonesome Echo." I couldn't figure out how we could buy an original Dali and not bust the seams of our budget. But I found out. His finished art was somewhat "limited" ... with the focal point being a colorful butterfly — cut from a book and pasted on the artwork. Dali wrote his interpretation as "the anguish of space and solitude," and signed it with a large flourish.

* * *

When I was a Capitol exec I used to argue with Marv Schwartz, our art director, who urged me to "get with it." He was right, of course — it was evident all around me. Some of the girls on the A & R floor were not wearing shoes. Or brassieres. Their see-through blouses I felt were disconcerting to the men working with them.

Not so, I was told. Young men take such things for granted and pay no attention. Apparently the girls wear such blouses for ventilation. The inference was that my dirty-old-man propensities were hanging out.

Maybe so. But all I can say is that if my secretary came in to take dictation in such an outfit I'd have to find it titillating. (Forgive me, Marilyn!) And I wouldn't be peering at her toes, which I must continue to regard as a strictly non-erogenous area.

Today, I wonder if the swing isn't back to preserving illusions. Grim reality is all around us. And coping with it, a daily challenge.

Maybe the market is ready again for covers with pretty girls, soft focus ... and colorful illusions to match the mood of the music. If so, I'm available!

* * *

In the middle fifties and sixties, all major record companies competed madly for Broadway show albums. Goddard Lieberson, president of Columbia, had the inside track, because he was an avid theater-goer, handsome and debonair on opening nights, with his lovely wife, Vera Zorina. He loved musical shows, and his company had a substantial bankroll to back up his convictions. For in those days, show producers were in a position to demand heavy investments in the show itself from record companies. In addition to which there was the album recording cost, and the cost of promoting it.

It was no business for petty gamblers or faint hearts. If a show flopped — and a majority did — the record company could lose amounts in six figures. One always hoped that he would recoup on the next show. And then we all felt it was good for our prestige, personal and company-wise. Perhaps Capitol wanted to prove it could afford to lose money just like Victor and Columbia!

I remember Lieberson even recording a group of old musicals, including "The Cat and the Fiddle," "Hit the Deck" and "Show Boat." I don't know if they made money, but I'm forever grateful because it's the kind of music I love, and play often.

As a Johnny-come-lately, Capitol had difficulty getting show albums. But then along came "Flaholey," starring the Peruvian princess, Yma Sumac, an artist under contract to Capitol. You may recall Miss Sumac's phenomenal voice — four octaves, from a rich sub-contralto to a crystal-clear soprano soaring to the stratosphere. We named her first album "The Voice of the Xtaby," a title based on an Inca legend — far more intriguing than the suggestion from our photographer, "The Inca Spots." The album was a smash bestseller for a long time.

So "Flaholey" was ours to record, because of Yma. I never did see the show because it closed before I could get to New York. The title was changed by our salesmen to "Flophooey" as it came back from the dealers by the truckload.

But then along came Meredith Willson's "Music Man" and Capitol's Broadway horizon was bright. Others followed, but this one show remains the classic for all time in the hearts of countless theater-goers.

A reverse twist on "Flaholey" was David Merrick's "Take Me Along." Merrick wanted Jackie Gleason for the lead — a Capitol artist under contract. But RCA had offered a substantial financial commitment for the show album. I wouldn't give up Gleason and Merrick wouldn't give up his cash advance.

As head of A & R it was my job to resolve the impasse, particularly since we would have an unhappy artist on our hands if Gleason didn't get the show. Merrick finally agreed he would give us his next available show, so I signed Gleason's release.

The show wasn't a flop, but it wasn't a hit either. I never could understand why, because I thought it delightful . . . with Walter Pidgeon, Robert Morse, Una Merkel, and other stars headed by the Great Gleason. How could it miss?

Merrick's next show was "Gypsy" with Ethel Merman. With bright eyes and high hopes I approached his office, ready to sign contracts. But this time he was involved with Columbia. I forget the details but it quickly became evident that there might never be a "next album" as far as Capitol was concerned. I had been outsmarted. And "Gypsy" was, as we all know, a great show, and recording.

As the years passed we released many more shows. Hits, near hits, disasters. Cole Porter's "Can Can" was a smash. "Fiorello," directed by George Abbott, with the songwriting team of Bock and Harnick, was very successful. It was followed by a musical by the same team — another great story and setting — "Tenderloin." I loved it. But Broadway audiences didn't. What a sad business.

Looking through my extensive collection of show albums, I find so many that arrived and departed like the BMT express. Good shows, some. Good writers, composers, and stars, mostly. For rarely is so much money invested with unknown talent added to the other hazards.

How quickly "flops" are forgotten by all, except probably their investors. "Greenwillow," "Gay Life," "Sail Away," "Wildcat," "Kean," "Christine," and many more . . . washed away in tears.

Yet money seems to be always available. For the smash successes are the ones that are talked about! "If I'd only had a piece of 'Pajama Game'." Or "Oklahoma," "South Pacific" . . . and always the immortal "My Fair Lady." What warming memories of the curtain rising on such stage and musical magic! Who knows when the curtain will rise on another? Where else can you get so much excitement for only a few hundred thousand dollars investment?

6

I guess I have always been plane crazy. I have never wanted to be a pilot; the very thought of learning about all those buttons in the cockpit and understanding the garbled static that seems so essential to survival terrifies me.

No, I was always content to travel on an expense account, enjoying the luxury of it all. In such fashion I have flown well over a million miles. And in almost every type of commercial plane and airline known to man.

Not too many years ago my traveling was limited to domestic flights from Los Angeles to Kansas City, Pittsburgh, New York and such. Outside of the U.S.A., I didn't know Fiji from Fuji. Then, when EMI, the English company, bought Capitol, I found myself leaping about the world with bewildered enthusiasm. Much of this book concerns the experiences I had in many countries . . . mostly after business hours.

There are of course, things that happened in the actual transaction of business abroad that are interesting — sometimes downright hilarious. But one hesitates to write about them for fear of offending worthy associates, who, with the best of intentions, were trying to beat me out of a legitimate profit in a miserable underhanded fashion.

I always traveled as a first-class passenger, except when I took my wife, Priscilla. One first-class fare, allowed by my employer, Capitol Records, almost paid for two coach seats. Thus I occasionally included Priscilla on trips to London, Tokyo and other places. And, as she squeezed into her coach seat, clutching her box lunch, I would sometimes tell her of the glories of the first-class section, so she wouldn't worry about my comfort when traveling alone.

Ah those endless cocktails. The stunning stewardesses. The gourmet food. The luxurious leisure, free from the tyranny of telephones. Never on land have I been treated so well.

Before I started traveling abroad, seat partners on domestic flights proved rather dull . . . ordinary people, doing ordinary things, just like me. When they found out I was in the recording business, some would complain about buying Capitol and Angel records and encountering bad surface noise.

I assured them such a situation was impossible, for we had quality control people . . . white-gloved virgins, who spot-checked records and could *hear* defects. Imperfect records were ground up for scrap.

But they went right on bleating about scratchy sounds. Occasionally I would send them replacement records.

Then one trip taught me a better technique. I learned to fight back! For this time my critic was the sales manager of a large cereal company. And I quickly complained bitterly about his Raisin Bran . . . the raisins were hard as pebbles, miserable little flavorless pellets.

"But that's impossible!" he protested. "We have a new process that keeps them tender and juicy!"

All I knew, I said, was that it was like eating bran mixed with gravel.

When I returned home from the trip, there was a whole complimentary case of Raisin Bran. And he spoke the truth, for his raisins were indeed succulent. I still eat the product, years later, and think kindly of him. For he got me off the defensive and I can now caustically criticize practically any product from Cadillacs to shoelaces . . . which are not long enough, wear out before your shoes do, and are hard to replace.

I recall when I had to go from my home in Los Angeles to New York every few weeks. When airlines announced movies en route I thought it would be great. But I quickly developed an intense dislike for this form of entertainment, born of a period when I made frequent trips and was exposed to an innocuous creampuff called "Tammy and the Doctor" three times. One could not escape, for there it was before you in all its fatuous flickering. I pulled out my earphones, but it didn't help because by that time I had learned most of the limited dialogue.

I read an ad recently stating that a major airline offered a piano lounge, with an opportunity, as they so wittily phrased it, to "tickle the ivories." My instrument was the banjo, and the only thing I could tickle would be the stewardess, but airlines have an archaic attitude toward such activities. Like the Playboy Club, where one is surrounded by overstuffed sex, yet one false move and you're out on your ear. My ear still hurts.

I have been asked on sundry occasions, when traveling, if I was married. My answer has always been a forthright and ringing "Yes!" For I have a theory — a conviction — which explains why happily married businessmen, such as I, become entangled in bits of activity involving g-i-r-l-s. I have expounded this on several occasions and have never yet met a traveling businessman who disagreed with me. In fact, several took notes as I talked, no doubt for later reference.

The facts, simply and honestly stated, are these: A traveling man who is "happily married" is loath to leave his wife in the first place. Thus, shortly after his departure from home, he misses her. This malaise grows more distressing as time passes and the miles of separation increase. And so, when our traveler looks into the limpid eyes of an airline hostess as she tenders his third martini — or, in those pre-panty-hose days, his eye happens to catch that nude area between stocking top and skirt hem, as she reaches high for a pillow across the aisle — we know, of course, what happens.

The traveler's mind turns to the girl he left behind. He is moved to tender thoughts. The young lady present epitomizes the affection and desire he feels for his wife.

I have been epitomized on many occasions. In fact, my deep devotion to Priscilla is such that I have been lonesome for her even before the plane took off the ground. Like that time in the L.A. Clipper Club, when the Tokyo flight was two hours late and Pan Am's lovely Brigette Zimmerman offered me cocktails, assorted nuts and sweet sympathy. Only my loyalty to our company, and my pressing need for an adequate income prevented me from canceling the flight and hurrying back home.

One wonders how such fundamentally wholesome motivations can so frequently be subject to baser interpretations.

* * *

Planes grew larger and more deluxe. The DC 3 was followed by TWA's Constellation, the DC 6 and the DC 7. I was a passenger on Pan Am's second DC 7 Polar Flight to Paris. Instead of going from Los Angeles through New York, it took the Great Circle Route, over the arctic. Now, it is routine, of course, but in those days it seemed fraught with excitement and danger. We all felt like pioneers.

I say "we" because two of my colleagues were along — Leo Kepler and Lou Schurrer. We waved goodbye to our families, and bravely stepped forward on the lush carpet through the lines of flags of all nations Pan Am had set up to signalize the event.

It was the day after Christmas, and we left California in brilliant sunshine, circled the blue sky over Catalina, and headed northeast. There were only three other passengers in first class, and only four in coach. No doubt most people, slaves of tradition, were remaining with their families during holiday week.

As we flew along all the goodies continued to come to us, served with great finesse, for this was a special flight, and Pan Am was giving its very best.

I glanced out of the window as I sipped my Manhattan. It was my third one ... perhaps my fourth ... who keeps count? A light snow was drifting past! I mentioned it to Lou, who was lapping up a Cutty and soda, on which I believe he was weaned. He asked me to call him if I saw Santa, heading back to the pole — he wanted to wave at Donder and Blitzen. We got to arguing about what the names of the other reindeer were. A stewardess came up with Dancer and Prancer, but that was as far as we ever got with the subject. And with her.

"Man, this is a *blizzard*!" Leo shouted across the aisle.

Living in Los Angeles, we had forgotten what snow looked like. From a plane window, it appeared menacing. We opened a map and estimated that we were somewhere over northern Canada, where Mounties plodded on snowshoes and sang stirring songs about love and duty.

Lou pointed to the small compartment near our seats labeled "Survival Kit" and suggested it contained a dehydrated St. Bernard dog with a small jug of instant brandy — you mix it with snow. We laughed. I wondered what *was* in it.

Then the captain came on the intercom. It seems we had been circling over a place called Frobisher, where we were supposed to refuel before "committing the plane to the North Atlantic." "I don't like that word, 'committing'," Lou muttered. I didn't either.

But Frobisher was "socked in" we were informed, and the only other refueling spot was Fort Churchill, over a thousand miles *back*. We were already headed for it.

The three of us huddled over a map. Frobisher was clearly marked, and it was indeed at land's end in the north. A bit of a bore it was, unwinding all that snow for the next two hours, but everyone agreed the captain showed good judgement.

But where was Fort Churchill? We asked the stewardess. She didn't know — they had never landed there. She went up to ask the captain, who, hopefully, was better informed.

It seems our destination was a town located on Hudson Bay. During the summer, when the ice melted, a considerable amount of grain was shipped from the port; in the winter everything was frozen solid.

Canadians, doubtless, regard Fort Churchill as we do Duluth. But our trio from California looked upon it as Admiral Peary country. Leo wondered, "If we missed Fort Churchill in the swirling snow, what then?" I later learned that had we been forced to touch down in the wasteland our chances of survival would have been slim. An SAS steward told me, on a subsequent trip, their crews were trained in arctic survival techniques — they could build a cozy igloo rapidly enough to avoid death from freezing for most of the passengers. The word "most" bothered me.

"Please fasten your seat belts," the Captain said about two hours later. "We are landing at Fort Churchill." We looked out of the window for twinkling town lights below. Nary a twinkle.

Down through the snow we came. Land leaped up at us, not a black and shining runway, but an expanse of glistening white snow. We landed and limped along to a stop. It was very dark.

Then, faintly, a distant light came on. It seems we had landed at a "Dew Line Base" where the U.S. Air Force was stationed. The pilot turned the nose wheel. When the plane stopped its bumpity-bump taxi trip we were in front of a lighted hangar. Our plane door swung open. And with it came the coldest blast of air I have ever experienced, before or since. I later learned it was 42° below zero, a temperature that was made more severe by the strong wind sweeping above the frozen miles of Hudson Bay.

Accompanying the wind came the largest and furriest Canadian Mounty I have ever seen. My only previous acquaintance with Mounties was at a performance of "Rose Marie," early in my youth. I recalled them in brilliant red uniforms exuding friendliness and good cheer. This chap was buried in thick furs. Only his eyes peered out, and they didn't seem very friendly.

I had carelessly neglected to bring my furs and earmuffs, but I did have a light gabardine topcoat which I scrambled into as I screamed a request to "shut the door!" We had the seats in front, and the door was right next to us.

Incredible as it seems, that Mounty insisted on checking every name on our manifest! It appeared we had landed, unscheduled in a foreign port, without authority. He had a routine to follow, lest some of us escape into the night, across the frozen wastelands. And after the name check, he insisted on checking the baggage lists — number of suitcases, boxes and such.

All this time the door remained wide open. Had it continued much longer all the passengers could more conveniently have been inventoried, frozen stiff and piled up neatly for tabulation.

In due course we staggered down the plane's steps into the icy blast, and stumbled across the chilling blackness of the airstrip. I had often heard the term "teeth chattering," but up to that moment I thought it was a figure of speech. Believe me, it isn't. My teeth were clacking like castanets, and I couldn't control them.

Lights glimmered in the night as we approached a building that looked like a military barracks, and was. We were ushered through several doors, like decompression chambers, ultimately arriving inside, where it must have been a cozy 50°.

We were in an American Air Force base. Most of the service men had traveled south for the holidays, so we were able to use their facilities. They were comfortable . . . a blazing fire and a Christmas tree. Both firewood and tree were flown up from the *south*, as we were far above the timberline.

Some two hours later we were told the plane was ready. Again we staggered through the frigid air, swathed in our Hollywood topcoats.

Warmed by the prospect of leaving this polar paradise, we fastened our seat belts and were taxied out for the take-off.

But back we came. It appeared that the nose-wheel had developed a flat spot that was "frozen in," making take-off hazardous. As I recall, it was one of the first neoprene synthetic rubber tires in use, and the problem had not been anticipated. Anyhow, we were forced to disembark and again we tottered our way back to the barracks, reeling in the wind.

One must say at this point that our crew persevered. I'm sure there was nothing in their service manual or experience to cover the situation, so their next gambit was a plan involving setting up a tent around the nose-wheel, then bringing in heaters to soften the tire to its normal contour. All this would take time, so we were scheduled to sleep in the barracks and would leave early in the morning. Pleasant dreams.

Our sleeping quarters comprised a dozen or so bunks in a room with heavily frosted windows. Having only hand luggage, there was no unpacking to do, so we stepped out to explore.

We were in quite a complex of buildings, connected by tunnels and protected walkways. The compound included a PX store, a movie theater, and other vital facilities.

All doors leading to the outside world comprised three small chambers. Judging by the furs, boots and such I saw in there, it was the custom to peel off layers of outer clothing in each compartment, ultimately arriving inside with nothing on but three sweaters and heavy pants, tucked into high, laced boots.

It was really arctic country. At the PX we were told that a polar bear had recently broken into a storehouse and carried off some goodies, leaving quite a mess behind. Some of the help looked like genuine Eskimos, right out of the *National Geographic*. I was intrigued to see an Eskimo child come in out of the cold and order an ice cream cone.

My eye was arrested by, of all things, a telephone. It was a typical pay phone, just like in your corner drugstore. Just for laughs, I lifted the receiver, dropped in a dime, and waited. A pleasant female voice inquired about my needs.

"Los Angeles, please," I said, giving the credit card number, area code and home phone in my best executive manner.

Click-click, tinkle-tinkle. My wife's voice! I suddenly didn't feel quite so remote.

"Where *are* you?" she asked, with a tone that seemed to infer I had slyly slipped off to Las Vegas.

Perhaps I milked the situation a bit too much. When I got through I had conveyed the impression that we were living off survival kits in hastily built igloos. It was not until she asked, "Igloos — with telephones?" that I was forced to come into sharper focus.

I learned later that when Gwen Schurrer, the wife of my colleague Lou, didn't hear from him she called Pan Am in L.A. They told her to call the San Francisco office. When she did this, she was told that Pan Am didn't know *where* the plane was! Seems incredible but that's what they said. Gwen began to worry.

Later, our explorations revealed the officers' bar, where a very courteous chap served us excellent drinks for twenty cents each. Flushed with the realization that this was eighty cents under L.A. prices, we accumulated over twelve dollars in savings in a relatively short time. This enthusiasm was later dampened when we learned that Pan Am would have picked up the tab for all drinks.

We ultimately retired to a small but well-set-up dining room with the other passengers. The food was sort of tea-roomish, but tolerable. All frozen, no doubt.

About the other passengers. As I said, there were only nine of them. Early in the voyage we found them worthy of but a casual glance. But now we made a more penetrating inventory.

First there was that middle-aged couple, who were perpetually grim and said absolutely nothing to anyone at any time.

Next, the lady with the small baby. Seems she was a prominent movie producer's wife, and was either running away from him, or traveling to him. Her contribution to the general gaiety was zero, but we got some smiles out of the baby.

Among those present was an elderly businessman, who yawned a good deal and didn't drink. A man of limited resources, we felt.

Then came three other people, who though not overgifted were adequate and typical.

I've saved the best for last. She was a stunning brunette in her mid-twenties. We all agreed that she brought out the best in our grooming and repartee. But she was as cold as a nose-wheel tire and as difficult to thaw out. In attempting to defrost her, all of us, singly and collectively, brought to this endeavor outstanding records of achievement. Alas, our most successful tried-and-true bits of badinage fell to the floor, and died without a quiver. Thereafter, we referred to her as "Miss Glacier."

Well ... nothing much to do now but go to bed. And we did. I drifted easily into sleep. It's one of the things I do best, for some reason. I have experienced personal tragedies that would make walking ghosts out of most people. Yet, as Priscilla has said to her mother, "Every time he gets horizontal, he falls asleep." Priscilla has difficulty in this area, puttering around the house after midnight and making noises that would awaken one of lesser stature. I know she watches the movie that follows the late-late show, because she occasionally relates the plot the next day, and tells me how handsome and gentle Leslie Howard was, or comments on the romantic baritone voice of Nelson

Eddy. Needless to say, our hour of rising also differs, and days can pass with relatively little contact, explaining, perhaps, why we do less quarreling than most couples.

Next morning we were told to pack up and board our plane. Even the gripping cold failed to freeze our jolly mood. Paris, here we come!

We scrambled up the steps and regained our seats. One by one, the motors roared into action. The plane taxied to one end of the runway, and with a great blast of power, hurtled down it for take-off and Gay Paree, no? . . . . No.

Brakes were jammed on, dishes and glassware crashed to the floor, and we came to a sudden, shuddering stop.

The pilot's door opened and the members of the crew headed outside. Soon they were back with a brief, apologetic report. The tire hadn't stuck on properly. The explanation was a bit cryptic, but I gathered we were to forego the immediate joys of the wild blue yonder to further savor the delights of Churchill.

The day wore on. Drinking had lost its appeal and we all got a bit edgy. Bedtime that night was nine thirty. What else?

But by midnight we were aroused, and again asked to hit the icy trail. Again we taxied down the runway for take-off position. But here the plane hesitated, as the Captain addressed us over the intercom, in a voice ringing with sincerity and confidence.

He wanted us to know there was no danger involved in this procedure. None whatsoever! While not exactly routine, it was nevertheless devoid of hazard. As an added fillip he stated that he had a lovely wife and children and wanted to get back to them "as much as *you* want to get back to your wives and children."

"I want to get to Paris," Lou said.

Again the motors roared. Again we raced hell-bent for the take-off point. But again we came to a shuddering, sickening stop.

Again, the bleak, freezing walk back to the chateau.

It was well after midnight, but none of the passengers wanted to sleep. We sat around staring at each other.

And then an amazing incident occurred. A real breakthrough!

Miss Glacier melted. The young lady turned to me, with a charming smile revealing perfect white teeth as she spoke:

"Let's play charades!"

I fought to regain composure as I answered, "Fine! Let's!" My colleagues suddenly assumed postures and expressions to convey that they were alive and willing.

Again she spoke, "*I* know a charade!"

I hesitated. As most of us know, that is not the way to play charades. Sides are usually chosen and the two groups huddle to select a subject that the opposite team must "act out," without speaking. Book titles like "Sex and the Single Girl." One of my finest moments was when I acted out "Encyclopaedia Britannica" for a twenty-second win. I *did* know the game.

But I didn't want to cool this chick — there was a long night ahead, and as senior executive in our trio I was entitled to some priority. So I replied, "Good! What is your charade?"

She told a little story: "There is a girl, stretched out on a bed, *stark naked*. On the floor by the bed is an empty bottle of whiskey."

It was an intriguing setting, and we waited eagerly for her to continue.

"What baseball term is it?"

I have been nonplussed before, but I must confess this was the nonplussest moment of my career. I looked at my colleagues. They wore anticipatory grins.

I looked at the businessman. He wasn't yawning. The lady with the baby just looked tired. The baby was asleep.

Then I looked at the couple who had neither spoken nor smiled since the start of this saga. They looked even grimmer. Didn't they like dirty jokes? The hell with them.

"I don't know — what baseball term is it?" I asked in my best straight-man style. With an impish grin, she replied.

"End of the fifth and no one on!"

Lou and Leo roared. Choked with laughter, they pounded each other on the back. A boff! A smash! The young lady glowed under their enthusiasm.

I glanced at the businessman. He was chuckling. Then I looked at the couple. The great stone faces were stonier than ever. They looked at me as if I were responsible for this vulgarity and Pan Am would hear about it.

The party blossomed. Lou discovered the sliding door behind the bar was not locked and since drinks were free to us anyhow, he felt no guilt in serving liberal portions.

Later, I learned two things, both significant. I found that the angry couple were from Sweden and didn't understand a single word of English. I don't know why they always looked angry. Perhaps they hated each other.

The girl of the baseball whimsy was a stewardess, deadheading her way to Italy for a holiday. Lou and Leo became instant experts on ancient and modern Rome. I watched them operate, with paternal amusement. Leo was more erudite, but Lou had the tenacity of a mongoose after a cobra. He expressed to me, when we finally went to bed, his deep concern over Capitol's business in Italy. He felt he should check into it. I agreed, but felt it sufficiently important to warrant my personal attention.

Oh, about the plane. Apparently top Pan Am officials came to the conclusion that it could not continue racing back and forth on frozen runways. And it was impractical to wait for the spring thaw; besides, the nose-wheel rim had been ground flat when it skidded along with the tire off. So another nose-wheel was commandeered from a DC 7 in San Francisco and flown up to Churchill in a *third* DC 7, thus tying up three of these large planes. I shudder when I think of the cost.

Even when the new wheel, with tire attached, was assembled, the captain *still* wasn't absolutely sure about the situation. In fact when we ultimately approached the runway at Paris, we landed like a praying mantis, on the rear wheels with nose held high. Then the nose came down with a thud. It was OK! A loud cheer went up.

We all lined up in the plane, eager to get out into the sunshine. But no ... we must wait. It was a long wait. Because this was Pan Am's Special Polar Flight, and they were busy rolling out a red carpet and placing chrome stanchions with flags of all nations fluttering from them. A crowd was gathering, under the impression, no doubt, that someone of importance was arriving. We finally staggered down the steps and limped through the glory of it all to customs. The Captain was there and waved goodbye, bringing to mind a poem I had been compelled to learn in my boyhood school days:

> Oh Captain, oh my Captain,
> This fearful trip is done.
> The ship has weathered every gale,
> The prize we sought is won!

As a final fillip, when we got to the hotel, there was a bottle of chilled champagne waiting in Lou's room — a gift from his friends, the Carlsons. We lapped it up with enthusiasm. Then, in a warm glow, I returned to my room and opened my suitcase. My glow cooled as I viewed a bottle of genuine maple syrup I was carrying to a friend in London. The icy weather in Churchill had frozen it, and broken the bottle. Upon thawing, the sticky stuff had slowly oozed through all my clothes.

7

In Europe, business customs and methods vary from country to country. But there is a broad similarity, perhaps because each nation is cheek-on-jowl with the next, and cultures overlap.

But Japan . . . there is a country that is genuinely *different* in every respect. In Japan a marketing man from America faces a facade of business activity very much like our own. But behind it lurks endless generations of tradition . . . a sort of big business feudalism that influences many of their attitudes and takes a lot of patient understanding from outsiders to conduct a successful business relationship.

But once that understanding is achieved, once you have proved to be considerate of their own persuasions and problems, business affairs usually run smoothly and to mutual profit.

At least that was my experience over a decade of activity in the Orient. And I must emphasize that in all my relationships with Japanese businessmen, I found them honorable and reasonable — once we figured out what the hell we were all talking about in our own peculiar languages and I had become accustomed to their methods of negotiating.

In my early business encounters in Japan, the long periods of silence were difficult for me. Sometimes we would all remain quiet for almost half an hour, and I would find myself dozing off or my mind wandering. I used to break into these periods of meditation with brisk phrases like "Well, let's get the show on the road!"

But later I sensed that the first one to open his big mouth lost face. So I developed a technique of working on my income tax problems, or other activities that would keep my mind occupied until they opened the next gambit, with "Now Mees-ter Doon. . . ."

Japanese techniques included a tendency to reach a basic understanding, with all participants sitting back in their chairs, relaxed. Then a new and higher officer would arrive. Appearing grieved at the generosity of subordinates, he would press for better terms. There was one senior executive whose figure would gradually slump as a member of his staff explained our agreement, until his head disappeared between his knees, and all you could hear were high-pitched moans of acute distress. I was alarmed when I first viewed this performance, but later accepted it as one would a glissade in a formal ballet.

My first business trip to Japan was memorable, for many reasons. I had been there perhaps forty years ago, as a young musician on a cruise ship. (And I must tell you, later on, how I split my head wide open on that venture!) So I was looking forward to dramatic changes. No more rickshaws, wooden sandals and such. And lots of opportunities for aggressive American businessmen.

I was in Copenhagen when I heard that Nat Cole was singing at the Latin Quarter in Tokyo. It seemed like a good time for my first visit, particularly since SAS had inaugurated a flight over the pole, direct to Japan.

Actually, there was little to do in Copenhagen, as Denmark was a relatively small market and I had already touched the necessary bases. But it was a weekend, and the city was, as always, a charming respite for a businessman. In fact, it is called "the Paris of the North." For me it has never quite lived up to that billing . . . no doubt my own fault, as I was once reminded by a charming young lady. I remember . . . it was a lazy Saturday morning, and I was lolling around in my room having a late breakfast with an American colleague in the hotel directly opposite the Tivoli — Denmark's Disneyland.

There was a rap on the door, and in came the maid to do our room. Now most hotel maids are old and frumpy, possibly to avoid arousing lustful thoughts among male guests. But this young lady was most attractive. And she spoke excellent English.

"Why," I asked her "do we find the night clubs all shut up in Copenhagen? Where do you go when you have a date?"

She informed me that nightlife in Copenhagen started at midnight, and continued on until dawn.

"But that's too late!" I protested. "How can people get to work the next day?"

She looked right at my gray hair and through my bifocals.

"We are young," she said.

* * *

One final memory of Copenhagen before we take off for the polar flight to Japan. There was a bus terminal off the hotel lobby, and in it was a kiosk for selling magazines. It featured, among other publications, some "girlie magazines" that were most revealing for those pre-porno days. When passing through I would sidle up to the display and indulge in a few surreptitious peaks. I had no idea that the young lady operating the stand observed me, but one day she peered round the kiosk, holding up a magazine she had extracted from below the counter. It was a *real* shocker.

"Here," she smiled. "This is much better!"

* * *

About that flight from Copenhagen to Tokyo. I believe it is the longest flight available on a commercial airline. Certainly it seemed so. We took off at an early hour and some time later landed at Bodo, Norway. No doubt you've been there. It's a tiny town in the northern part of Norway — which is about as far as you can go and still gas up a plane. A few people live there, very few. I got off the plane, stretched my legs, looked around, and got back on — having seen all there was to see. Again we took off, going directly over the North Pole, as distinguished from other polar flights, which fly a thousand miles to the south. I do believe somebody should put a marker at the pole — it would be a kick to see it from a comfortable spot above.

After another five hours I strolled up to the lounge to break the boredom.

There she was, playing solitaire . . . a Nordic beauty if I ever saw one. I've always been fascinated by the game, so I sat opposite her and offered some helpful suggestions. We had a drink or three and in no time she was laughing gaily at my witticisms and calling me Lloyd. It was wonderful to encounter a woman with such a highly developed sense of humor.

It was really a delightful tête-à-tête. On several occasions the huge, handsome SAS captain passed by and gave me a sly smile, indicating his approval of my selectivity. Time passed rapidly and I was surprised to hear the announcement that we were landing in Anchorage to refuel.

Much to my surprise, my lovely companion announced that she was getting off at this Alaskan outpost. Having been to the place before, I came up with a rather good *bon mot*. "What's a beautiful girl like you doing in a dump like this?"

"I live here," she said. "My husband is the captain of this plane."

All I could think of was the story of the guy in the barber shop trying to date the manicurist. He asked if she was married. "Yes," she said. "My husband is shaving you."

* * *

Having nothing better to do in Anchorage I wandered about the airport waiting for my plane to refuel, for the long, dull trip ahead. The Anchorage airport had all the charm and capacity of one that might be operated in Moose Jaw, Montana. The need for refueling polar flights had overwhelmed the place into a seething sea of planes and people.

The waiting room was jammed and hot, and there was no place to go in the short time available. I finally decided to have a shoeshine because I could thus sit down for a few minutes.

The man who operated the franchise turned out to be a black gentleman from the deep south. I asked him, "What in the world brought you to this cold climate?"

"Money," he replied. When I paid a dollar for the shine, and saw the line waiting for the chair, he made sense.

The only shoeshine that cost me more was in "The Phone Booth," a restaurant in L.A. featuring "topless" ladies. One entered through a conventional phone booth on the street that had a back door. There, a well-endowed topless girl stood by a sign reading "Shoe shine — $1.50." The price was high, but my shoes *were* dusty, so I placed one foot on her portable stand, resenting the group of freeloaders who clustered about. She shined it, I must say, with considerable vigor, but then demanded a *second* $1.50 for the other shoe, pointing out that the sign said "*Shoe* shine," singular! It was a bit of brazen effrontery that my audience particularly enjoyed. I joined the group awaiting the next victim.

*   *   *

I arrived in Tokyo in the early evening. (God knows what it was in Copenhagen time!) I was dead tired, but a group of enthusiasts met me at the airport, led by Warren Birkenhead, "our man in Tokyo," and Carlos Gastel, Nat Cole's manager. The town *had* changed. It was brassy and big and loaded with enticements for "men with yen," to quote a book title on the subject.

Carlos Gastel was a fat, happy Latin, and a gracious host. As I write about him I recall a story that I found moving . . . and frustrating, too.

Carlos was in Hong Kong, and visiting Aberdeen, where the famed "floating restaurants" feature exotic seafood and other goodies. It is a well-known tourist attraction. The barges are beautifully illuminated, reflecting flashing lights in the dark waters of evening. These restaurants are reached by sampans — little floating taxis, propelled by one oar off the stern of the boat.

The sampan that took Carlos and his companions to the barge was operated by a young Chinese woman, who twisted her oar with vigor and expertise. At the bow of the boat, in the tiny living quarters, was a small boy of perhaps seven years. He was studying a schoolbook by the dim light of an old oil lamp.

Carlos wondered about the boy. He was her son? And the boy's father? Who knows. The mother worked the taxi to get food and keep the boy in school, no doubt.

The dinner was splendid and so were the large number of martinis and the wine Carlos consumed. On the return trip to the pier, his group coincidentally got the same sampan.

It was quite late. But the little boy was still studying under the dim lamplight.

Carlos was deeply touched. By the time the sampan reached the dock, he had worked himself up into an emotional state about the dedication of the mother and the application of the boy to his studies.

He paid the fare — a trifling amount. Then he removed an American *one hundred dollar bill* from his wallet and placed it in the woman's hand as he gestured toward the boy.

"For the lil feller's ed-cashun," he said thickly, as he tottered up on the dock.

This story might not be worth the telling were it not for the woman's immediate reaction. She looked at the bill. She crumpled it up. And she threw it violently at Carlos, standing on the dock.

Then she pulled her oar out of the water and swung it at Carlos. It caught him on his broad backside and sent him sprawling.

His friends stared in disbelief as the woman thrust the oar back in the water and vigorously paddled off.

Nobody knows exactly why this action took place. The most plausible explanation came from a man who had lived in Hong Kong many years.

"She thought your chap wanted to buy her son," he said, "for immoral purposes. It's done here, you know."

Carlos' reaction was sad to behold. But I think the most tragic aspect was the opportunity missed by the sampan lady. A hundred dollars represented many months' labor. It would have cared for her son in a good school for perhaps a year. And she would have realized that there are nice people in this world who do good and kind things, expecting nothing in return.

I sometimes wonder where those two tiny souls are today . . . swallowed up in that mass of humanity. I have a nice feeling that the boy has done well, and his mother no longer needs to paddle her own sampan.

*   *   *

There are many aspects of Japan that are perhaps worth recounting. Their whole system of doing business is different from ours. When young graduates join a large company, they are locked in for life. Thus the company takes on a paternal role, and cares for them in many ways unknown in the U.S.A. . . . where one can be greeted any morning by a boss who snarls, "Git your ass outa here — you're fired!"

The Japanese system has obvious advantages, but limits opportunity for individual growth. It is difficult to shift from one company to another, as American executives do, collecting substantial increases, bonuses and stock options in the process. But the young people seem uniformly eager, hard working, determined to do a good job. And, most important, happy.

Perhaps I am overdramatizing it, but to me their faces shine with eagerness. Never was that more apparent than when I stood back stage at the Latin Quarter while Nat Cole sang to a large, young audience. Peering through the curtain's folds I could see hundreds of eyes glowing like Christmas lights, sheer delight reflected in their faces as he sang by rote, in Japanese, a love song that involved pointing to individuals in the audience . . . "Like you . . . and you . . . and you." When he finished, there was a burst of applause — no screaming, squealing, leaping up — just polite, respectful approval.

Today our cultures have so intermingled that young audiences' reactions are more volatile. I suppose performers like it better that way. I find it one, of many, sad indications of "progress." Surely the way Nat's audience looked at him was sufficiently expressive to be amply satisfying.

Yet, to this day, audiences in Italy throw rotten vegetables at opera singers who displease them. Races and customs differ . . . that's what makes traveling so fascinating.

EMI-Capitol owns a record company in Japan with Toshiba, a large and world-famous organization which produces a great variety of products. I was instrumental in setting up our 50-50 deal, one of the first in Japan after the war. I became a director of Toshiba Music, Inc. and attended most of their monthly meetings. The whole affair was conducted in Japanese, so my presence was merely a legality. But I had been well briefed by Warren Birkenhead, an America engineer who lived in Tokyo, spoke good Japanese, and looked after our interests. So I sat at the board table, trying to look intelligent, and staring at my nameplate in front of me. You may have a mild academic interest in how Lloyd W. Dunn looks in Japanese. (As I understand it, only the "W" could not be translated.) Here it is:

取締役　　ロイド・W・ダン

I'm convinced that airlines have an automatic "categorizer." When they push my number, out comes DOB, for Dirty Old Businessman. I am usually placed with a seat partner who is male, dull, smokes cigars, and talks too much without saying anything. But occasionally there are some strange variations. Not good, but different.

Like a flight I once took on a Lockheed Electra KLM from Amsterdam to Athens, where I had a business appointment.

We left at 10:00 A.M. As we were snapping on our safety belts, I glanced at my seat partner. He was a man, perhaps in his late thirties, nicely groomed, and looking a bit grim.

We had barely gotten off the ground when he touched his call button. The steward, a nice-looking young chap with blond curly hair and a courteous demeanor, stepped up. My seat partner wanted a martini.

"And you, sir?" the steward asked. Now, I am usually capable of holding my own in such activities . . . but at ten in the morning? "Coffee," I said. "Black."

As my seat partner gulped his martini he started to explain. He was a doctor, from Aberdeen, Scotland. He owned a house on the water, near Athens, and once a year spent his vacation there. "I know it sounds silly," he told me, "but flying terrifies me. So I prescribe for myself . . . three martinis on take-off. It gives me Dutch courage!"

At lunchtime, I joined him in a libation or two, and I learned that he spoke Greek and knew Athens intimately. I told him I was staying only one night in Athens, transacting business the following day, and in the early evening taking off for, God help me, Singapore, over 4000 miles away. I mentioned that I regretted not having sleeping pills with me, because I would surely need them on that endless flight.

The good doctor had some pills in a medical kit he carried in his suitcase. He suggested we meet at a small cafe near my hotel, the

Grand Bretagne, where we could have a few drinks and he would give me the medication.

In a further conversation I mentioned my love of Greek bouzouki music. The bouzouki looks like a long-necked mandolin, but it is amplified and has a loud, happy sound. He knew a place in Piraeus, the seaport of Athens, where such music was played, so I invited him to be my guest for dinner there. It was a very pleasant flight, chatting with him.

In Athens I showered, shaved and put on my other business suit. I found the doctor relaxing at a sidewalk cafe, sipping ouzo — a Greek liqueur that looks like dishwater, has a licorice taste and carries considerable authority. He was in an open-collared shirt wearing a vivid blazer, carrying the emblem of his university.

The chap he was sitting with looked vaguely familiar. Then I remembered . . . he was the steward on our flight from Amsterdam. A moment later another young man joined us. He was introduced as a tourist guide in Athens, apparently a friend of the doctor. We were all to have dinner together.

I was mildly annoyed, because I had invited the doctor to dinner and was now involved with financing a party of four. But . . . what the hell. We all squeezed into a cab and headed for the waterfront.

It was then I noticed something strange. I was seated in one of those "jump seats" that are pulled down. The tourist guide was on the other one. The doctor and the steward were close together on the rear seat, where the good doctor had his arm around the boy's neck and was running his fingers through his golden curls. The steward's eyes were closed and he leaned back in a state of complete relaxation.

I am not very astute but the picture became suddenly clear. The Greek boy was *my* date for the evening.

Conversation froze and my stomach soured. Never, in our discussions during the flight was there a hint of such inclinations. And now — to include *me* in such an assignation!

I know that today "gay lib" and such activities have changed many attitudes. I suppose every man has a right to his own way of life, without censure. But I had been leering at ladies since the age of five, when the little girl across the street took off all her clothes and sat on a sprinkler head.

The rest of the evening was one I prefer to forget. I ate little and drank a good deal, but remained cold sober. They permitted me to pay all expenses, including the cab ride home.

The next night, on my flight to Singapore, I realized that the doctor had not given me the sleeping pills. I was wide awake all the way to Bangkok.

* * *

Before leaving this subject, I must comment about an incident that occurred when we lived in Bel Air. Next door to us were two men — one a successful screen writer and the other his male "housekeeper." Priscilla used to chat with him occasionally, and one day he told her they were leaving for Europe. She offered to care for their cat.

"Oh no, we're taking him with us," he said.

She asked *why*?

He replied, "Because he's never been!"

* * *

I had another kind of silly experience on a trip from Honolulu to Tokyo. It was one of the early flights of Pan Am's huge 747, and it had a full load. It had all the charm of traveling in the lobby of the New York Hilton.

Not being familiar with the configuration, I had asked for a window seat in the nonsmoking section. They readily complied and when I got on the plane I found out why. My first-class seat was close beside a battery of toilets. On a 747 there are quite a lot of them.

My seat companion was a nice-looking woman, perhaps in her middle forties, with a dignified and slightly aloof demeanor. Always the gentleman, I offered her my window-seat, which she accepted. This placed me somewhat closer to the washrooms, where if I bulged out too far in the aisle I would be sideswiped by the traffic.

The flight droned on its endless hours. After drinks and dinner there was a noticeable pickup in attendance at the local facilities. Having nothing better to occupy my mind, I found myself engaged in what researchers would entitle, "length of occupancy by type and sex."

It became quite intriguing. I pulled up my sleeve to expose my watch for more accurate timing. I began to do rather well at it, making only one really bad estimate. This chap entered, carrying a shaving kit — a good five-minute man if I ever saw one. But when he emerged there had been barely enough time for vertical bodily functioning. Puzzling.

There was a tugging at my sleeve. "What in the world are you doing?" the lady beside me asked.

Lacking a more socially acceptable explanation, I told her the truth. She, too, became intrigued. Having no experience, her estimates were somewhat naive, but she showed promise. A short while later, we were making book on the activity at ten cents a visit. She tried valiantly, but when we quit, several hours later, I was well ahead.

* * *

One doesn't get to sit next to intriguing, colorful people on planes very often. My seatmates are too frequently elderly dullards, almost as old as I am. Ladies in this group were of such limited potential that I never recall burnishing even my substandard opening gambits.

However, I can't say I haven't had at least a few interesting partners on planes. Like the fellow on a flight from Singapore to Hong Kong. He was an exceedingly well-groomed gentleman with a neatly trimmed mustache and an alert demeanor. I learned he was a major sales executive for Ovaltine, a well-known product you will recall as a cocoa-like powder, recommended for its soporific qualities at bedtime — most certainly an innocuous potion. It was therefore startling to learn from my seatmate that China was a major market for this product. When I asked *why*, the gentleman's answer was even more amazing.

It seemed older Chinese gentlemen believed Ovaltine to be an *aphrodisiac*. S'help me, that's what the man said. They mixed the powder with a little water, eating it with a spoon . . . or perhaps chopsticks, though I can't imagine how. Then fun, fun, fun. It shows how much of that sort of activity starts in the mind. He didn't know what Ovaltine salesman had created the myth. But I assumed he hadn't taken steps to dispel it.

His stature among the Chinese was obvious, when I found his picture on the front page of the Hong Kong newspaper next morning, flanked by a glowing group of greeters.

Strange, Capitol has for years been attributing aphrodisiacal qualities to certain recordings, with limited sales in the Orient. Jackie Gleason was a master proponent. He called his first album "Music for Lovers Only," and carefully specified the setting for the cover photograph . . . a handsome coffee table in a lush apartment, on which rested a lady's handbag, gloves, and an ashtray with two cigarettes, one tinged with crimson lipstick . . . and both still glowing . . . as, no doubt, were the smokers, who had retired to another room.

Today, I can't imagine trying to coax a young lady into the sack to the pounding roar of electric guitars, but I don't really know.

Oh, about Ovaltine. Believe me, it's no help.

* * *

I moved on from Hong Kong to Tokyo on JAL — Japan Air Lines — where I had a first-class seat, with the one next to me empty. But just before taking off, it was taken by a Chinese woman, perhaps in her late fifties, wearing one of those black peasant outfits you see in the outlying country, as you approach the borders to Red China. She sat staring straight ahead, motionless.

JAL's service is always lavish, and I was plied with cocktails and exotic hors d'oeuvres shortly after take-off, which I sipped and munched happily. Then I was suddenly aware that the lady beside me had received none of these goodies. A moment later, when the lovely Japanese hostess tendered me the elaborate dinner menu, I noticed that she did not offer one to the Chinese lady.

I stepped up forward and asked the hostess "How come?" She said the woman was a coach passenger. They had moved her up next to me because all seats were taken in the rear section. Under such circumstances they could not, obviously, serve her anything.

I visualized for a moment, the picture of Dunn, the ugly American, gobbling and swilling endless offerings, while the lady sat beside me without even a small bowl of rice.

So I told the hostess that I *insisted* she serve the lady exactly what I would receive. Since they had seated her in first class beside me, the present situation was untenable. She told me that it was not possible.

"Then I must insist that you stop serving me," I told her. This was not a gesture on my part, to impress anyone. I just found it all most embarrassing. The hostess bowed politely and disappeared in the pilot's cockpit, up front.

Shortly thereafter, she appeared with magnificent trays of food for me and for the Chinese lady. I chomped away happily, in a warm glow of virtue and achievement.

Then I noticed the Chinese lady. She was back tight against her seat, staring wide-eyed at the tray before her as though they had brought her a live cobra, ready to strike.

Throughout the entire meal, which I ate with decreasing enjoyment, she never touched anything. In fact, she never moved a muscle.

I surmised later that she came from a humble background and couldn't imagine what all this *was*, and why it had been given to *her*. Perhaps she thought she was going to have to pay for it. I will never know.

As I sat there uneasily, I did wonder what the attitude of the hostess would be when she came to collect the trays. I can imagine the snide I-told-you-so remarks I would get from an American girl under such circumstances.

But when the lovely young lady in the kimono appeared, she was expressionless. She offered me after-dinner drinks with grace and charm, without a hint of rebuke. I am sure that is one reason why I fell in love so easily, and frequently, with Japanese girls.

* * *

I had mentioned sleeper planes, which are no longer available. TWA had one — a real luxury flight to Europe. The handsomely appointed Constellation accepted only 25 passengers, all of whom had seats in the rear and beds up forward. And all this for only fifty dollars above the regular fare!

My last venture with a flying sleeper was on SAS's flight from Copenhagen to New York. Priscilla was traveling with me and we had a lower sleeper, which was amply wide enough for two.

When the plane left at eleven, one hour late, we immediately slipped into night clothes and drifted into dreamland, lulled by the drone of the plane's engines.

Slightly over two hours later, we were aroused, and told we were going to refuel at Reykjavik, in Iceland. I told the hostess to go ahead and refuel — I hadn't even a mild academic interest in the process. But it seems the law states that passengers must leave the plane during refueling. So we were compelled to dress, stagger out into snowy, below-zero weather, and wait in a Quonset hut, where coffee and native artifacts were available for purchase.

Returning to the plane we found our bunk made up. It was explained to us that it was hardly worthwhile for us to undress and get to sleep, inasmuch as breakfast would soon be served. It seemed reasonable.

During our scrambled eggs, Priscilla and I amused ourselves by estimating that the hundred dollars extra fare for the bed made sleeping pretty expensive — around a dollar a minute. Small wonder that this service was shortly thereafter discontinued.

*   *   *

My first memory of flying was in the early 1930's. It was a very small commercial airline that ran from New York to Philadelphia and on to Washington. I remember being quite nervous as I climbed into — well, I can't recall the kind of plane, but it was maroon and seated about twelve, with the pilots sharing the open cabin, where you see them and hear them, and sweat out the flight with them.

After we took off and gained our altitude — I suppose about 5,000 feet — it began to rain. And *how* it rained! I had assumed that planes don't work well in heavy rain, because the air is all cluttered up with water. I began to get twitchy. But we bounced along and finally made the Philadelphia airport. Here we landed for a weather check and refueling.

The pilot waited a while, but finally decided to continue on. There were fewer passengers, and I wondered if some had dropped out as a matter of judgment or destination.

When we got up into the air, it was not only raining harder, but was windy and rough. I was trying to look unconcerned and casual, but my performance was not of Academy Award stature.

A while later we landed. Much to my surprise I discovered it was still Philadelphia. We waited in the airport while the plane was refueled and pilot reassessed the weather conditions.

During the wait, I reassessed my own condition, for more passengers were dropping out. I figured that when one elects to stay in Philadelphia, the situation was indeed precarious. But my mission was pressing.

I was in love. Desperately, painfully, awfully in love, as only a very young man can be. How wonderful it was, as I look back through the years. It was long before the era of youthful sophistication and cynicism. I asked simply for *approval.* Let me be *with her* for those few precious hours before I must turn around and head back to the family flat in Brooklyn.

I wonder if any of my three sons — ages 18, 20, and 25, as I write this, and unmarried — will ever experience such "agony and ecstasy." Perhaps it has gone out of style. I do know that it was an experience that to this day, many decades later, sometimes creeps out of my subconscious and takes over my elderly dreams in anachronistic realism.

Her name was Mary Houston. In New York there is a subway station by that name and the conductor always bellowed *"House*-ton Street!" when the train pulled in. But she told me it was *Hugh*-ston . . . in her dulcet southern accent, so sweet in contrast to the familiar Bronx and Brooklynese that surrounded me. She was the daughter of the City Manager of Fredericksburg, Virginia — a lovely and historically prominent town south of Washington, D.C. I met her through Wilson Wilmer, a chap who worked in an art studio where I was an apprentice, and who later married my sister. He was from the south, and Mary, his cousin, was visiting his parents.

I had recently been on a trip through the Orient. I had played in the orchestra on a cruise ship, the *President Lincoln.* And I was determined to work it into the conversation, to impress her. For in those days few people traveled, and to many my trip was the equivalent of a lunar expedition today.

We were dancing in a Chinese restaurant on Flatbush Avenue. Overhead, the huge colored glass chandelier turned slowly, and myriad tints of light drifted across her lovely face. I recall the exact conversation . . . amazing after all these years, when today I can't remember my phone number.

I said, "That's quite a trip for you, coming here all the way from Virginia. As a matter of fact, I recently took a trip. To Shanghai. That's in China. I just got back."

Now I expected her to say "China? How exciting!" But instead, she looked up at me with those deep purple eyes, and snuggled a bit closer as she said, "How lucky for me."

This was my first direct exposure to the coquetry of the southern belle, famous in story and song.

I melted. I *dissolved.* The tender tendrils of love imprisoned me from that magic moment . . . for a long, long time thereafter.

Like the song in "Pinafore," I was a common sailor and she the captain's daughter. And the Great Depression was beginning to gain daily headlines and breadlines. All those and many other things I weighed against a love that possessed my every waking moment, and followed into my dreams.

And that's why I was on the plane, stranded in Philadelphia. It's also why I quickly determined to fly on, come what may.

71

Of course, we arrived in Washington safe and sound. From there, I took a two-hour bus trip south. She was there, waiting, and we became engaged to be married.

I took many such trips in the two years following, but usually on the train because it was cheaper. It left New York at midnight and arrived in Washington at 6:00 A.M. with a connecting train to Fredericksburg, that puffed into the station at 8:00. At 4:00 P.M. the same day, I reversed the process and headed back. It was a long journey, but the special excursion rate was only five dollars and, need I say, was worth it.

My last trip to Fredericksburg, I will never forget. The train arrived at 8:00 A.M., and we went to her house. There she told me she wanted to break the engagement . . . it was all too hopeless, and she had been going out with other boys, and felt it wasn't fair to me . . . or something along those lines. I understood only one thing. It was over.

I was a proud young man. And I guess I had known for a long time that socially, financially, and geographically, I was doomed. All I said was, "When does the next train leave?"

Twenty minutes later I was on it, headed back to Brooklyn. I had the world's longest train ride ahead of me. I sat there, hour after hour, trying to put it all in a perspective that I could live with . . . endure.

From out of the past drifted a few of Longfellow's lines, from my schooldays in English 11 . . .

Talk not of wasted affection, affection never was wasted.
If it enrich not the heart of another, its waters returning
Back to the springs, like the rain, shall fill them full of refreshment;
That which the fountain sends forth returns again to the fountain.

Then, like the boy in the Japanese song "Lonely Fool," I walked the streets of New York . . . looking up at the stars, so the tears would not run down my face. It's hard to see the stars in New York.

9

I have sometimes been asked the question, "What kind of music do *you* like?"

My answer, I am sure, is not in the best taste. I always say, "The kind of music I like is music that *sells*." It is an attitude essential to survival in the record business, and any executive that humors his inclinations to please his ear rather than his pocketbook is doomed to disaster.

Classical music comes to mind as a real problem area. Symphonies, for example, used to cost from twenty thousand dollars up to record. Operas, perhaps seventy to eighty thousand on occasions when problems developed . . . as they frequently did.

One of EMI's most illustrious Board members once got me aside and talked for an hour on the desirability of recording chamber music. He loved it, and felt everybody else should. The fact was that chamber music, while relatively inexpensive to record, had such a limited sale that it was sure to lose money. And this gentleman was very much profit-minded . . . as all good directors should be.

The major problem with classical music is that the same works are done over and over, different only in the conductor, orchestra, or soloists. Capitol has, for example, three complete "Carmen"'s in its active catalog — by Bumbry, de los Angeles and Callas. There are also a few "Carmen"'s of older vintage reposing in EMI's inactive catalog. And a great many more "Carmen"'s have been issued by RCA, DGG, London and many other companies. Every year adds to this list.

The reason, of course, is that "Carmen" is perhaps the most popular and saleable opera. Yet very few record-buyers would pay for more than one — perhaps two — versions. So every catalog competes with itself and with a dozen competitors.

David Bicknell was worldwide head of classical recording for EMI. He

73

is a rare person ... tall, a roundish, reddish face, with large, blue, ingenuous eyes. His gentle voice and unassailable logic has calmed many a tempestuous meeting of executives, artists, producers, conductors, and others involved in recordings.

Among my other duties I was at that time head of Angel records, in America. So I was very much a part of EMI's activity in classical recording.

Our English colleagues organized a group called ICRC — International Classical Recording Committee. Executives from the major classical markets, notably U.S., U.K., Germany, France, and Italy (and later, Japan) met twice a year in London to decide on recording programs that would be saleable, profitable, and hopefully, "an artistic triumph," to quote David.

In operas we had to work perhaps two years ahead; getting the right conductor, soloists and orchestras together involved frightening logistics.

First we had to decide on a work that offered some remote possibility of selling enough in a five-year period to return its recording cost and some slight reward to our shareholders. In desperation, one time, someone came up with "Fidelio," Beethoven's only opera. There had been no new recording of it in some years. When we did it, we found out why. It is not a popular opera.

Once a title is selected there is the problem of casting it. It makes the recording a lot easier if the soprano and tenor do not completely loathe each other ... thus assuring that they will make sweet harmonies instead of shouting obscenities at each other in several languages, while a huge orchestra politely waits, secure in the knowledge that such debates result in extra profitable sessions.

Sometimes the conductor joins in the imbroglio, while the EMI producer, whose future security depends on getting the recording done with the greatest dispatch, dances nervously about the participants, making conciliatory noises as the relentless hands of the clock move on with "nothing in the groove."

I was surely the ICRC member who knew the least about classical music. But I had one of the biggest voices as head of the largest market area. So I'd try to conceal my ignorance as names and titles were tossed about the table and recommendations made. My participation was frequently confined to two questions.

"What will it cost to record?"

"How many will it sell?"

This usually put a stop to aspirations to record some obscure work that would be an "artistic triumph" but a financial disaster. We'd frequently wind up doing things like another version of "Cav and Pag" ("Cavelleria Rusticana" and "Pagliacci"). Both are short operas, together requiring only six LP sides.

ICRC meetings were, in a few respects, like auctions. A work would be selected, with suggested artists. Then we would go around the table to get estimated sales figures.

America? "Fifteen thousand."

U.K.? "Ten."

Germany? "Maybe five."

France? "We'll import a few."

And on it went. When all bids were in, we'd add them up, figure the costs of recording, packaging and such — then estimate profit. Frequently there wasn't any.

Speaking of "Carmen," there was one recording that was well remembered at EMI for the problems involved. When in London recently I asked David Bicknell to recount the story which involves so many of the emotional, musical and financial hazards of such a production. His writing is restrained and undoubtedly soft-pedals the pandemonium, but it is colorful and historically accurate — so I quote it in its entirety:

> You have asked me to recount what I remember of the troubles which arose when we recorded "Carmen" in Paris with Victoria de los Angeles as Carmen and Sir Thomas Beecham as conductor. It was in 1958. Here are the facts as I remember them; these troubles were serious for the Company but some moments were farcical.
>
> That the recording had been suspended became general knowledge and was the subject of much lively speculation in the American musical press who recounted with many picturesque details indicating that there had been a first class row between Victoria and Sir Thomas over the interpretation of the part, etc. This was quite untrue. They had the greatest admiration for one another as musicians and had made some years earlier a recording of "La Bohème" in New York for us which was one of the most successful operatic recordings since the War and is still a favourite in the record catalogue.
>
> The "Carmen" troubles arose from a totally different cause — the illness of Sir Thomas's wife Betty who was with him in Paris and died a few weeks later in Buenos Aires. Beecham, like so many other great conductors of his generation, was blessed not only with a first class brain which retained its clarity, as I can testify from personal experience, until the last week of his life, but also a wonderful physical constitution. He undertook and carried out a programme of work which would have exhausted many a man half his age. But in Paris he over-taxed even his iron constitution. This arose from the fact that the recording of "Carmen" in Paris' Salle Wagram came at the end of a concert tour when he was already tired, but also when the illness of his wife, which

became progressively worse, prevented him from getting the rest essential to a man of 79 so that he became rapidly more and more exhausted and irritable.

The practical consequences were a disorganized recording schedule, the tiring of the singers and a general mood of frustration and exasperation.

Victor Olof — and none was more experienced in this field — was in charge of the recording and I remained in London. Victor warned me by telephone that the programme was getting more and more behind schedule and it was unlikely that it would be finished before Sir Thomas had to leave to conduct a season of opera at the Teatro Colon at Buenos Aires and Victoria travel to the San Francisco Opera where she was engaged to sing Desdemona in Verdi's "Otello."

Things came to a head when one evening Victoria's husband, Enrique Magrina, rang me up to say that she could not put up with the disorder any longer and was off to Barcelona to rest and allow her voice to return to its normal pitch before going to America. I asked her to stay one more day but the most that I could persuade her to do was to meet me for half an hour at the Paris Airport before flying home.

When we met I found that she was more frustrated and tired than angry and she convinced me that there was no point in her staying any longer as the opera could not have been completed by her doing so. My last question was, "Have you told Sir Thomas?" She replied that she had tried to do so but could not find him on the preceding evening when she had made her decision and she asked me to break the news to him. On this note we parted amicably and I drove straight to the Hotel Rafael in Paris — a hotel near the Arc de Triomphe where Beecham often stayed when working in Paris.

I went up to his suite and found him with his American manager, Andrew Schulhof — an old friend of mine. Sir Thomas's first question was "Where is Carmen? I want to have a talk with her about our next session." I looked at my watch and replied "I think that if the plane is on time, she is just touching down at Barcelona Airport."

I never saw a man more dumbfounded. After a moment's silence he said, "You mean she has walked out without telling me?"

I said, "No, she tried to tell you and she has asked me to explain her reason for going." He then blew up as I expected he would do, saying angrily, "I have never been treated in such a manner during my fifty years in the opera house."

There then occurred a ludicrous interlude which although

unplanned, helped to reduce the temperature. A French waiter, mistaking the number of the suite and without knocking, threw open the double doors of the suite and pushed in a trolley table loaded with an elaborate luncheon ordered by someone else, crying cheerily, "Bonjour, messieurs, bonjour!" All Sir Thomas's wrath fell on this wretched man who found himself face to face with a furious, old and formidable gentleman dressed in an open-necked white silk shirt, red suspenders and baggy sky-blue trousers (very much the cut of a French railway porter), who shook his fist in his face and finished a tirade in French by shouting "Get out" in English. He disappeared at the gallop with his trolley shedding, as he went, bits of Toast Melba, like the leaves in autumn.

I started to laugh at this disappearing apparition and Sir Thomas, whose sense of humour was never far away, started to laugh too. So we parted in good humour.

But to get the opera on the rails again was another matter. I heard the tapes which were, to my surprise, very good. All the same I thought that rather than run the risk of another confrontation between two great artists for whom I had, like so many others, the greatest respect and affection, that it would be better to stop and write off our considerable financial investment. So I wrote to Sir Thomas in Buenos Aires saying so.

He replied that he had no intention of stopping and that he would discuss the matter with me when he returned to London. This we did. Good sense prevailed on all sides. Victoria flew specially to London to meet him and found that he was restored to health and good spirits. So new dates were arranged and the recording brought to a triumphant conclusion.

Most buyers of the records — and they have been bought in tens of thousands all over the world — have no idea that at one time, in place of this lyrical, graceful and dramatic interpretation of Bizet's masterpiece, it looked as though only molten paving stones would emerge from the Salle Wagram.

I would like to stress, all the same, that this was by no means a unique occasion when recording opera. The strains on all participators are always great and Wilhelm Furtwangler, for example, stormed out of the great recording of "Tristan and Isolde" with Kirsten Flagstad over an incident which now seems in retrospect quite trivial, and it took the efforts of all of us but particularly his charming wife Elizabeth, to get him going again.

* * *

Maria Callas ... now there is a woman! Colorful, tempestuous, talented, attractive, fascinating ... and unpredictable. She had tremendous box office appeal and still does.

One time, I had the pleasure of joining Maria for dinner at the Plaza in New York. John Coveney, Capitol's artists' relations manager, was our host. John was tall, suave, handsome — and an expert in his field, which included calming Italian tenors. He rode over the turbulent waves of opera stars' flareups like a well-groomed hydrofoil, beloved and respected by everyone as he soothed shattered nerves and patched up strained relationships.

I knew that my knowledge of opera was, to put it kindly, limited. John knew it, too. But I was hoping our secret would not be shared by Madame Callas. With only three of us at the table, I could not lean back in my chair with an erudite sneer, a gambit I occasionally used at major classical meetings in London. She would surely think me an idiot.

John said not to worry. If I felt insecure, have another drink.

The moment arrived when we entered the handsome dining room. The glamorous Maria aroused a buzz of ohs and ahs as we progressed toward our table. ("That's John Coveney with her — but who's that elderly chap, trailing behind?")

Maria was utterly charming. We drank champagne, discussed investments, politics and other miscellaneous subjects. It was only when I reached my hotel room, late in the evening, that I realized not one word had been said about opera. Whether this was due to John's adroit manipulation of the conversation or her shrewd perception and consideration, I will never know. Probably both.

Opera buffs will recall that Callas had a falling out with Bing, and did not sing in New York for several years. Then came the announcement that she would return to the "Met" for two performances of "Tosca," the first of them a gala benefit for the Metropolitan Opera Guild. The town was agog, and tickets were impossible to obtain at any price.

On the evening of the Gala, I arrived at the opera house in a rented Cadillac, with tuxedo to match. The huge crowd at the entrance pressed close, looking for celebrities. I bent my head slightly as I stepped out of the car, hoping to be mistaken for somebody important. I did succeed in arousing considerable interest. For my snap-on black tie popped off into the surging throng. And getting it back was only possible when the recipient, who caught it mid-air, realized that as a souvenir it was worthless, and tossed it back. I slunk into the opera house, found my seat, and witnessed a major Callas triumph.

I remember how dramatically Maria's basic compassion was evident when one evening in an earlier season she was singing with a young tenor. There was a portion of a duet where he was required to sing alone, without orchestra — no doubt expressing his undying love as he wanders around in the high register for perhaps sixteen bars, eventually returning to the note where he is rejoined by Callas for a flourishing finish.

The only trouble was he had wandered too far afield. It became obvious to almost every member of the packed audience that he had departed from the original key and would nevermore return to join in glowing harmonies with Callas and the orchestra.

The question before the house was "which way will Callas go?" Would she join him, to assure sweet harmony . . . or follow the orchestra, when the conductor brought down his baton to bring forth an instrumental blast in a different key? Either way assured a musical disaster.

All I can recall is Callas, doing a masterly job of wrestling the wandering tenor into the right pitch in a scant two or three bars, placing her face close to his in apparent loving tenderness. They both finished with the orchestra in grand style. I don't think the tenor was ever aware of what had happened.

But opera audiences are notoriously critical. Their enthusiasm — and their displeasure — can be deafening. At the Met, vegetables are not thrown, as in parts of Italy. But they do hiss and boo in a pretty frightening fashion on occasion. Thus my heart ached for the young man when his moment came to step on the stage alone to take his bow, following Maria's ovation.

But Callas never left his side! Thus the crowd was forced to include him in their wild acclaim for their beloved Maria. I suppose there were some in the audience who resented this gesture, as Romans at the Colosseum might if a Centurion wrapped a protective arm around a Christian when the lions appeared. But I suspect the majority approved what she did, and loved her the more for it. I did.

I was in England recently, invited to EMI's 75th Anniversary party. The London Symphony played. Yehudi Menuhin performed. But the fun party was the small dinner held at the new Selfridge Hotel, owned by EMI. I was a guest speaker, and noting the smug glow of satisfaction on the faces of my former colleagues I said, "I hope you gentlemen haven't done anything so vulgar as to make money in the classical music business?" I was quickly informed — practically in unison — that the classical division was now one of EMI's most profitable activities! It all seems to have happened since my retirement. Embarrassing.

* * *

In fairness, I was not completely at a loss in classical music — particularly in the instrumental area. I had played a rather pathetic cello in small orchestras. But my classical career began with the bass viol.

I was a high school student in Brooklyn at the time. The head of the music department encouraged me to play the bass, because of my height, and the orchestra's desperate need. One hour every day, I practiced alone in a small airless room adjoining the auditorium, following the "ten easy steps" offered in an instruction book I bought for a dollar. As I think back, I made amazing progress . . . when one is young and eager, learning seems such an easy process. In a relatively short time I appeared with the orchestra, as the lone bass player, standing tall in the background, and grunting away in the lower register.

We played all the standard overtures, but the one that bugged me was "The Marriage of Figaro." It opened on about eight bars of a fast phrase that was rapidly performed by the entire string section in *absolute unison.* Then it moves on to a more melodic passage, where the bass part repeated the same low note, which I pumped with ease and grace. But the beginning — I just couldn't cut it. At public appearances, standing there stark and exposed, I developed a technique of moving my fingers rapidly, and pumping the bow arm. But I kept the bow a full inch above the strings where it could do no harm, and was not visible to the audience.

And I kept practicing that opening phrase. Over and over and over I practiced it in that hot little anteroom. And one day at rehearsal I was emboldened to touch the bow to the strings and join in.

The conductor, Dr. Yerby, was an elderly gentleman who no doubt had Toscanini-like aspirations in his youth. He stood before us, a saddened man, and his face reflected the genuine suffering he must have endured as he marked the beat. But apparently the limit had been reached for he raised his head and tapped vigorously on the music stand. The orchestra came to a scratchy halt. He pointed his stick at me in a rapier-like thrust. I will never forget his words.

"Dunn," he said, "I don't mind you wiggling your fingers. But for God's sake keep that bow off the strings!"

10

I wanted to tell you about how I split my head. It really happened. It was split right down the middle, starting slowly and gradually widening until the whole thing was loose and flapping.

It happened a long time ago, when I was a young man, but I have never forgotten it. Because it generated a highly awkward situation, and almost spoiled my first trip to the Orient.

I was living in Hollywood, working as an assistant script writer for Pathé serials. This art form probably started with "The Perils of Pauline," and became very popular, not only with the kids but also with many adults. Even in South America, Pearl White, who played Pauline, was the reigning pin-up girl. Those were the days before talkies, so titles could be easily changed into other languages. Thus *"Se fue alla,"* was an easy translation for "He went thataway!"

Actually, the stories were so elementary that titles were unnecessary. There were, of course, the bad guys and the good guys. The bad ones were easy to tell, because they had mustaches, and were always lurking about peering around corners and smirking evilly.

We usually had the same leading man in every serial so he was easy to identify as a good guy. On several occasions I tried to write him in as a bad guy pretending to be virtuous in the early episodes, but everyone was horrified with the idea. We had sort of a stock company, and everyone knew his place. Our leading "heavy" was Frank Lacteen, a real nice chap who was so constantly making evil grimaces that it must have been difficult for him to look pleasant when he arrived home after work and kissed his wife.

There were a few variations in leading men. We used Gene Tunney once, just before he fought Dempsey. He wasn't much of an actor, and he used to bewilder the company by spouting Shakespeare, but he did become World's Champion as the picture was released, and it was recut into a feature called "The Fighting Marine." I doubt if even the late, late show on TV would accept it today, so don't sit up.

I should mention that Spencer Gordon Bennet (one "t" please!), the director, was my uncle. He started in the business as a stunt man. When the company was located back east, he had to jump off a cliff and into the Hudson River far below. There was a rowboat there to pick him up after the scene. But he landed too close to the rowboat, and the splash knocked it over, tossing the two occupants into the water. One couldn't swim, so Spence wound up rescuing him ... which was not in the script. He is still in fine physical shape at 80, and plays competitive squash.

I started my movie career as a "script girl." Women were always used for such jobs, so when I took it over, in a gesture of nepotism, the company insisted on regarding me as a *girl*. When we were on location, they had a trailer with toilet facilities for the women, which was used by the ladies of the cast, while the men disappeared behind rocks and bushes. Great efforts were always made to get me into the car with the ladies. I was young and shy, I suppose, and it was good fun for the gang.

But I was a washout as a script girl. My job was to keep track of the scenes and action for the director. For example, when the girl ran into the old shack at the waterfront to escape, and six of the bad guys followed her in, we would shoot the exterior at San Pedro, and weeks later we'd do the interior on a studio set. I then had to remember the order in which the bad guys entered the door and details of dress, so the interior shot — a direct cut — could match. After several startling scenes when the man with the beard ran in the door *first*, and showed up inside *last*, with a different coat on, I was removed from the assignment, and made a reader in the script department. Here, at least, I could use the men's room with vertical dignity, but I missed the action on location.

People were always chasing *something* in serials ... the Rajah's ruby, the "papers," the Treasure Map, and such. We were late with a shooting script once, an original story called "The Black Box." Throughout fifteen episodes, good and bad guys madly pursued The Black Box. But we did not reveal *why*, because no one knew what was in it ... least of all the guys writing the script.

I remember saying to Joe Roach, my boss, with genuine concern, "What could possibly be in that box that would justify fifteen episodes of all this chasing around and killing?" He didn't know, and looked very sad about it as he pointed out that this was a chance for my youthful ingenuity and maybe I'd get screen credit.

We finished the serial without *anybody* opening the box. The leading man clutched it to his bosom and said dramatically, "There are documents in here that could plunge our country into war with evil foreign powers!" It was pretty feeble, and I apologize to the kids, now grown, for letting them down.

In the light of today's pornographia it is interesting to recall that while our leading lady was always lovely, with her coiffure undisturbed after a five-mile chase and an underwater swim to escape from the hangout, she was *never* sexually molested, nor was it even suggested, in a drooling closeup. One would think that the *first* thing such abject villains would do when they got the girl in their power would be to rape her. But no — they tied her up to a chair, gagged her, and started to drink and play poker, thus proving to our young audience how very bad they were. None of that sissy stuff. In fact the male lead didn't kiss our heroine until the tag scene at the end, when we usually faded out on their simpering closeups, to avoid loud kissing noises our audiences frequently indulged in, to show their contempt for such a silly business.

But then came the day when we had apparently produced enough serials for the immediate market, for we were all laid off. My brother, Lin, who was always the eager-beaver type, promptly wrote a letter to the American President Lines (then called the Dollar Line) stating that he had a fine, organized orchestra and would accept an engagement to play on one of their cruises to the Orient. I told him it was a waste of time — who would read a letter, scribbled by some kid nobody had ever heard of? But he lacked my sophistication and was always doing things like that. In fact he still does. How he ever got to be a top Hollywood cameraman in the special effects field, puzzles me.

But we got an answer in the form of a telegram from San Francisco, asking us to visit the *President Lincoln* for a tryout when it reached Los Angeles — in two days! Of course we had no orchestra. But we knew enough musicians, none of whom were free for the cruise but were available for the tryout.

We were accepted for the trip, and fortunately no record was made of who was playing what. Because, as it turned out, I was the only one who made the trip. Lin suddenly landed a job as a first cameraman and could not turn down the opportunity. He had been the second cameraman for several years, which involved setting his lenses as the first cameraman directed, and having nothing to do with lighting and framing the shots. Lin's negative was used for foreign prints. Now he would take over all these responsibilities. It was too good to resist.

I madly beat the bushes to get an orchestra together. How I did this is a story in itself, but sufficient to say I appeared at sailing time with an orchestra of sorts, urging them to act like old buddies, who had been playing together for years. There were five in the band — piano, sax, violin, drums — and me. We'd had about a half hour's rehearsal, but I had received a pile of stock orchestrations, and the boat was stuck with us, once we passed under the Golden Gate. As leader of the orchestra I received $45 ... not a week, but every month. The four garden-variety musicians under me got only $40.

It turned out that the violinist, who doubled alto sax, and the tenor sax, were quite good, and nice chaps. The drummer was affable too, but lacked sensitivity and whacked away with vague abandon.

But the pianist ... there's the rub. He had a certain school-learned technique, but without printed music in front of him, he was *dead* — couldn't fake the simplest songs passengers would request. And the music the publishers had given me turned out to be all their old orchestrations of tunes that never made it. The situation was desperate.

Even worse, the pianist turned out to be an enthusiastic homosexual ... which certain members of the crew quickly discovered. I had only a vague idea that there were such things, in that Age of Innocence, and was bewildered when I stepped into our little cabin, below deck in the crew's quarters, to find my pianist in bed with a large and very ugly "able-bodied seaman."

It took the rest of our orchestra to break up this romance, during which we bruised the pianist a bit ... not too much, because he had to play later in the day.

Actually, before sailing we had listened to a stern lecture on S-E-X, by a Dollar Line official. The substance of his talk seemed to be that we were a nice clean bunch of boys, and were to stay away from *all girls* in the Orient. He dramatized his words with graphic illustrations of exposed gentlemen, whose private parts were in various stages of decomposition, all ghastly. It scared me so that when I went ashore in Shanghai, I walked down the middle of Nanking Road with both hands in my pockets, and an alert eye out to ward off rapacious females. But I was not molested, except for a small boy who tugged at my sleeve and suggested, in American vernacular that he had obviously learned by rote, that I engage in a quite intimate relationship with his sister.

I must relate one story about Shanghai that in perspective suggests a good reason why modern China evolved. Our group had just stepped off the *Lincoln*'s shore boat on what is called "The Bund." Unlike most waterfronts, which are shabby, this was a handsome area in the International Section. On a nearby corner was an impressive hotel, and from it wafted delightful music. It was early evening, and a group of Chinese people had gathered in the street before the hotel's large bay window, to listen. We walked up behind them and stood there, enjoying the fine string orchestra playing a Strauss waltz.

But suddenly there was a mad scramble with screams of pain as the Chinese broke and ran. A large, bearded and turbaned Sikh policeman had charged into the group, wielding a truncheon, which he used in a highly professional manner to beat off the music lovers. We backed away in alarm, but stopped when he smiled and gestured us toward the now unoccupied view directly in front of the window.

It seems that we, as white people, were entitled to every priority. When we had first approached the hotel window, the Chinese should have backed away to permit us a close and unobstructed view. The fact that these people, entranced with the music, were not even aware of our arrival behind them, did not mitigate their offense.

Later, I noticed a lovely park with a sign, "No Foreigners Allowed." I learned that in this application, "foreigners" meant Chinese.

*   *   *

But I have wandered afield. I wanted to tell you about splitting my head, while playing in the ship's orchestra.

Perhaps I haven't mentioned that during the dinner hour, I played the cello. I didn't play it well, because I had never taken any lessons, but I could manage the simpler selections that didn't leap up too high on the fingerboard into thumb positions, and I was devoted to the instrument because of its sweet, poignant tone.

But when the time came for dancing, I switched to the banjo, on which I was more comfortable and qualified. In those days, before amplification, banjos were used for rhythm because they had a crisp, loud tone and could cut through the attempts of saxes and brass to drown them out. In addition to the standard thumping technique, I could leap about the fingerboard in a few single string routines that aroused mild acclaim among the missionaries aboard ship, who were headed for the Orient to Spread the Word.

Our first stop had been in Hawaii, which I must say I found exquisite. I still do, today, despite too many fat ladies in muumuus and elderly gentlemen in Aloha shirts, soliciting heart attacks. And in those days there were no high-rise hotels blocking the natural beauty.

As our boat departed from Honolulu at sunset, we were on deck, softly playing the Aloha. The passengers dropped their flowered leis in the water, and watched them drift away in the shimmering wake. Then a full moon came up, and with it a gorgeous *moon* rainbow, sweeping the sky in a pastel glory.

It was the loveliest thing I had ever seen. And yet . . . incomplete. I remembered Sara Teasdale's lines:

> Oh beauty, are you not enough?
> Why am I searching after love?

That evening I lavished my love on a cello solo . . . the "Evening Star" from "Tannhauser." The divers applauded politely, no doubt unaware of the extra quiver in my vibrato.

*   *   *

Every time the ship left port, the orchestra was required to play on deck, for the departing passengers and their guests. As the voyage progressed we began to derive a sadistic pleasure in softly playing melodies like "Til We Meet Again" and others that incorporated sad sweet thoughts involving the possibility that those concerned might *never* meet again, life being what it is. People who came aboard to bid farewell to friends and relatives, wept copiously, stimulating us to even greater efforts.

Once an elderly lady, reduced to a sobbing, semi-hysterical state, hit me with a large purse as she screamed, "Stop that music!" It was a great tribute, we all agreed.

* * *

Almost halfway between Hawaii and Japan, the head of my banjo started to split. It comprised a circular piece of treated animal hide, drawn taut on its metal frame, and responsible for the staccato, lively tone of the instrument. Probably the damp sea air got to it, or maybe it was dying of old age after endless battering. In any event, I watched in horror as the split continued and the sound was reduced to a tubby, toneless flub.

Thus, when we reached Yokohama I had only one objective: *get a new banjo head*!

I don't know whether you've ever tried to purchase a banjo head in Yokohama, but let me assure you it presented problems. Today the Japanese make practically everything. But this was over forty years ago, with rickshaws for transportation, wooden shoes clicking on cobblestone streets, and very little English spoken anywhere.

Had I wanted to purchase an obvious item like shoestrings, it would have been difficult. But my shopping expedition seemed hopeless from the start.

I approached one of the more affable looking rickshaw-pullers and opened the banjo case. I showed him the large split in the head and made sounds and gestures indicating my dilemma.

I was pleased to find him sympathetic and eager to help. In fact I gathered that he knew a place specializing in banjo heads. With hopes high, I climbed into his cart, clutching my banjo close as he went galloping off into the rising sun.

After perhaps twenty minutes he stopped before a quaint-looking building with many oriental embellishments. It didn't look like the sort of place that would vend banjo heads, but after all this was Japan, where things were obviously different. I clambered out of the cart and approached the handsomely carved and varnished door.

It opened before I reached it, and out came some very lovely girls in kimonos, chattering and giggling like the Three Little Maids in the "Mikado." I was charmed but puzzled. I showed them my broken banjo head. They were also charmed but puzzled.

It took some doing before I realized that this was an institution devoted to satisfying the carnal cravings of seafaring men. I was wearing the ship's uniform, and when I had engaged the rickshaw, the man took me where every sailor went after a sea voyage. The banjo? Well, he knew foreigners had strange customs and perversions.

I returned to the rickshaw and addressed the man with rising emotion. I reopened the banjo case, shouting "Music! Music!" and sadly shaking my head as I traced the break with my finger.

Ah — *this* time he understood! Again we pushed forward. But in due course we came to an establishment that looked surprisingly like the first one. It was. Only in this one the girls played music!

When I left Yokohama, my head was still splitting. The capital city of Tokyo had nothing to offer, and that held out little hope for Kobe, a smaller industrial city and our next stop. I'm afraid I did not enjoy the beauties as we sailed through the Inland Sea, for the purser was beginning to regard my situation as an act of sabotage, and my status as an orchestra leader was rapidly dropping ... understandable when one remembers that our pianist could not fake music and I had been holding the orchestra together with vigorous rhythmic effects, to answer requests for old college songs and the like. My poignant cello added little to our dance ensemble.

At Kobe I repeated my routine, for I could think of nothing else to do. Again, the affable rickshaw man understood, and we bounded forward into the unknown. But this time we continued on, far beyond the city limits and into spreading farmland. There were no stores around of any sort, and he ignored my efforts to stop and renegotiate the whole excursion.

I began to feel that I would soon be thumped on the head and left in a rice paddy, to slowly sink into oblivion.

Then he stopped before a small cottage. Without hope, but at his enthusiastic urging, I entered it ... thinking that if this proves to be another Japanese whorehouse, I'll bash him with my banjo and leave *him* sinking into a rice paddy.

I was greeted by a smiling kimono-clad gentleman, surrounded by the square skins used on samisens, the instruments you've seen geishas plucking in those lovely Japanese prints. He eyed my broken head with professional interest and — wonder of wonders — came up with a perfect banjo head carrying the stamp of Rogers, a Chicago manufacturer. Where, how and why he got it, I have no idea.

Banjo heads must be dampened and stretched as they are applied, so the process took some time, during which neighboring farmers came in to admire the instrument, and, apparently, look at me. When the work was finished I hit a few chords and played a tune to test it out ... and was greeted by a burst of polite applause. I gave them my best encore, "The World Is Waiting for the Sunrise," which was even more enthusiastically received. Tea and biscuits were served. It was all most warming, particularly the price, which was under the going rate in Chicago and New York.

I left in my rickshaw, to the courteous bows of the group, and we trotted off back toward the city, where I regained my ship and my status, as we sailed out of Kobe at sunset, into the Yellow Sea.

Bless you, rickshaw man . . . may your bowl of rice always be full to overflowing!

11

Today, many tourists have visited Russia and know the "Intourist" routine . . . wherein never was a guided tour more guided.

Intourist, for those who have not been to the U.S.S.R., is a sort of government tourist agency. Complete tour tickets must be bought and paid for before arriving in the country. Businessmen and tourists are handled alike. One has no idea in what hotel he will be deposited, which makes communication from the home office difficult.

The whole routine of being "processed" is unlike that in any other part of the world — time-consuming, fraught with hazards and puzzling. I'm sure the Russians have good reasons for every laborious step, but it does take some "getting used to." For a businessman, it must take several trips before he knows his way around, up and over the complexities. Perhaps it is different today — my trip was a few years ago. I hope so.

Take money, for example. I had been warned that the Russians are very strict about it, for they are maintaining the stability of the ruble through government control . . . and this takes a bit of doing. You must account for every penny when you enter the country. You have prepaid your hotels and meals, so all money spent must be verified when you leave, with bills and chits. Changing money at other than the fixed rate is illegal, with serious penalties involved. This puzzled me because shady looking personages frequently contact foreigners right in front of hotels with offers of money-changing at favorable rates. It seems to me that such activities must be quite obvious to the local police and that a labor force for the salt mines was within easy grasp. But there they were, operating in the open.

My son Jeffrey had been studying Russian in high school and college. Under the assumption that he could at least come up with such phrases as "Where is the men's room?" I brought him along to Moscow during his summer vacation. Capitol had been negotiating a contract with the U.S.S.R. to release their great classical recordings in America on our Angel label. The artists were of top rank — the Oistrakhs, father and son, Richter, Rastropavitch, Gilels and many others. But business activities that were routine in other countries were difficult here. I am quite sure the Russian executives wanted to be cooperative, but there were a great many traditions and limitations that slowed things up to a creeping crawl.

For one thing, I don't believe they are ever sure of the area of their responsibilities. In the U.S.A. we have job descriptions. In the U.S.S.R. everything is interlocked, and ultimately moves on up to some mysterious controlling force. Even opinions are not expressed by minor officials. It kind of bugs an American businessman who is used to going to the mat and wrestling out a decision. But you accept it when you realize that everyone is trying to do a good job within his area of operation.

After arriving at the Moscow airport, and being "processed," we were delivered to a staggeringly huge new hotel named "The Russia," but called the "Comrade Hilton" by the local wits. It must have incorporated many thousand rooms, but when we were there a large portion was still under construction, which perhaps explains the limited services available. The ultra-modern architecture of the structure stands in anachronistic contrast to the dramatic historic structures of the Kremlin across the square. But one does not criticize.

We entered the tremendous lobby and sought to register. Behind a large curved desk were quite a number of what we would call room clerks. In front of each was a long — very long — line of prospective guests waiting to register. These were not just ordinary lines, such as one encounters at an American hotel during the first day of a Shriners' Convention. The Russians were obviously offering a new refinement. Every so often, a desk clerk would shift position — and with him would go the line of people who had picked him in their earlier Russian-roulette-ish choice. As there were many lines, they would intermingle as they swayed with the tide of events, and participants fought to hold or improve their positions.

Ultimately I had my golden moment standing before a middle-aged plumpish lady in black. She indicated that she spoke no English. From her point of view our relationship had ended. I looked about desperately for son Jeffrey, to justify the expense of bringing him. He was nowhere in sight.

Before selecting a new line, I edged toward the desk and listened, selecting a clerk who spoke English. Then I retreated to a back position among her faithful followers. Again, after a long wait, I arrived with a hopeful smile, as I extended my Intourist card, given me at the airport.

She glanced at it and said, "I do not register your room number." When I asked her who *did* she pointed back to the lady who spoke no English. End of conversation.

My voice rose in quivering eloquence, while those behind me in line twitched restlessly, regarding me as a troublemaker. Anticipating being tossed from line to line for endless hours, I refused to move. Let them send me to the salt mines!

Ultimately she took compassion on me and handled the necessary paperwork, by the simple expedient of walking over to her colleague's desk and locating my documents. It was complicated only by the surging line that moved back and forth with her. We were then escorted to a small suite that was modern and very comfortable.

I am sure that conditions in Russia have improved since our visit, but at that time I can only say things were "peculiar." For example, the next day we were greeted in the lobby by our Intourist guide, a slim, attractive and energetic young lady. I informed her that I must get to the office of — and here I showed her a letterhead — Mezhdunarodnaya Kniga. (Jeffrey says it translates into International Book, but I don't quite trust him.) This was the division of the government devoted to the arts, including music and records. I was due there at ten o'clock for a meeting.

Our guide professed to never have heard of Mezh Kniga (called this, for "short"). She didn't know the address. Her attitude suggested we drop the matter and get on with proper sightseeing, or she'd inform the authorities.

I explained our business involvements and suggested she get a phonebook. She disappeared for a considerable period then returned, without the book, or even an explanation. A while later I concluded that there is no phonebook in Moscow. Perhaps it's considered too informative. (P.S. I just talked to a colleague, Bob Myers, who has since made several trips to Moscow and he has never yet encountered a phonebook!)

I checked their letterhead from my correspondence for an address or phone number. It had neither. Our letters to them merely said "Moscow," where apparently the postman knows his route.

The situation was at a ridiculous impasse. Then I used an age-old gambit. I consulted the international source of all information — a cab driver. In other countries, the question might be "Where's the action?" In Moscow it was "Where's Mezh Kniga?" *He knew.*

And off we drove. S'help me it wasn't half a mile away — we could see it from the hotel: a huge, old office building, the largest in Moscow. And nobody knew where it was!

I wondered about the guide. Perhaps she had never been assigned to a businessman and was suspicious when I didn't ask to see the Kremlin and Lenin's Tomb, across the square.

When we arrived at the building, our guide was not permitted to enter with us. Ultimately we were ushered into a large room with a big oak table, where I sat in quiet solitude.

Then the door opened and a small group of gentlemen entered and greeted me cordially. Someone opened a box of chocolates, strange to me at a 10:00 A.M. business meeting, and we nibbled at them as we talked. One or two spoke fair English, and translated for the others. I don't know why I should have anticipated otherwise, but they turned out to be nice, friendly people, trying to do a job within the obvious strangling limitations drawn for them by some official edict.

I soon determined that business decisions in Russia are never — but *never* — made on the spot. And certainly never by an individual, at least not by the ones I contacted. Copious notes were always made for later reference and ultimately, some decisions were forthcoming. When they disapproved of or could not fulfill my request, nothing was said. The word "no" is not used in business discussions there any more than in Japan, where American businessmen have lolled in night clubs, feeling they were making genuine progress in their mission, only to ultimately discover that their offerings had been rejected at the first encounter. In Tokyo, I believe a direct "no" is considered impolite, in contrast to the American way, where we lean back on our chairs, hold our heads in derision and say, "You've got to be kidding!" or, "I wouldn't touch it with an eleven-foot pole!" In Tokyo they say "Hah-so!" which could mean anything, but usually means nothing. I would translate it as "Hmm-m-m."

Later I had another meeting with a group of the creative recording branch of Mezh Kniga, headed by a large, impressive chairman wearing many decorations and a very stern expression. He spoke no English and his attitude reminded me of Groucho Marx's old song, "Whatever It Is, I'm Against It!" Unfair, I'm sure, for so many of these people speak only Russian and have never been out of their country or had any real executive experience.

An interpreter was supplied for us, who in addition to studying the language, was a college music major. I remember one demand made by the Chairman, which I hoped I understood, as translated. They wanted their trademark "Melodiya" to appear on every album cover in exactly the way they had designed it. Perhaps this trademark had been developed to appeal to foreigners by an artist who had never been out of Omsk. It was styled like the lettering found on jars of cheap cosmetics, lacking the virility and character I felt was needed to lend the proper exotic appeal in the U.S.A.

So I carefully explained to our interpreter in my best diplomatic language how much I admired their trademark, and how clever it was for them to conceive it. Left to naught but my personal taste, I would use it with satisfaction and great happiness. But under commercial pressures, I was forced to conclude — etc. and etc.

My interpreter translated my poignant appeal into a relatively few words, which produced an angry expression on the Russian's face. Later Jeff explained that my eloquent and understanding phrases had been reduced to the direct statement, *"He won't do it!"*

I was finally reduced to a somewhat unfair stratagem as I said to the interpreter, "Will you inform the Chairman that if he is adamant, I will follow his instructions. But he must then realize that the responsibility for success or failure — profit or loss — then will rest on *his* shoulders, not mine."

It was ridiculous of course, but effective. For no Russian wants to take ultimate responsibility. The Chairman was a good poker player; his expression never changed as he listened. Then he spoke. The interpreter told me, "He will think about it."

I went ahead and redesigned the Melodiya label in the most effective style for our market. I guess he is still thinking about it. The Angel-Melodiya line was a great success, due, I am sure, to the superb musical performances.

As time passed, we developed a better rapport with the Russians, granting it is a relative term. I remember when they told me it was the 50th anniversary of the U.S.S.R. They wanted all their records in America to carry an embossed gold seal bearing the slogan, "Fifty Years of Soviet Power."

I pointed out, delicately, that such a slogan might be unappealing — even frightening — to many Americans, who bought a great many classical albums. We changed it to "Fifty Years of Soviet Music."

I feel that I developed a warm relation with the Russian businessmen, although documentation would be difficult. It seems that their friendly gestures were mysteriously impersonal. For example, Jeff and I took a brief trip to Leningrad. Tourists buy first- and second-class tickets for their entire trip, a bit contrary to Soviet political philosophy.

When our Aeroflot plane landed in Leningrad, we were escorted to a hotel of ancient elegance, in the center of the city. Most impressive was our very handsome suite, and even more overwhelming was the concert size, brand-new grand piano in the living room! It was a Beckstein, made in Austria, and considered by many to be among the world's finest.

Jeff sat down, delighted, and played for an hour, while I nipped at a small bottle of vodka which I carry for emergency use. It was a delightful respite for both of us. And I will always be grateful, for I am sure it was prearranged by the gentlemen from Mezh Kniga, who knew of my son's musical background. Surely few hotel rooms in Russia — in the world — are so equipped. Perhaps the suite is normally occupied by opera stars and instrumental soloists, for Leningrad is a center for such activities.

An Intourist guide was supplied us in Leningrad, another charming young lady who pointed out areas where beautiful objects used to be before they were purchased by "American millionaires." Even a highly decorative metal fence was included — we saw the spot where it used to stand. And at the Hermitage, when we commented on the vast collection of great masters, she said, "There were more, but they were purchased by American millionaires." What a greedy group of capitalists we must have been. I wondered how Russia accumulated all those Rembrandts, but didn't dare ask. Russian millionaires, perhaps?

Jeff then distinguished himself by losing his plane tickets, which would ultimately take him home to California. This is the sort of thing one laughs about today, but at that time the humorous aspects were not as readily apparent, as I paid for a new set. Ultimately the airlines involved refunded the money. Except Aeroflot. I'm sure they wanted to, but the paperwork was just too overwhelming, and to me, an American millionaire, the amount trifling.

I mustn't leave Russia without mentioning that I am a balalaika buff. I love the tinkling tones of this musical instrument and I was eager to hear them in the country of their origin. I also wanted to buy one for my collection, which includes a bouzouki from Greece, and other native instruments from various parts of the world.

But the only balalaikas I could find were at Gums, the huge department store in Moscow. These were cheap in price and poor in quality, having obviously been mass-produced for tourists to take back as wall decorations.

As for balalaika music, I was finally informed I could hear it only in a night club, at the Hotel Metropole. Jeff and I strolled over there one evening, finally locating a room that contained a long table and wooden benches. A bit spartan for a festive place, but let's not get so critical of everything, I told Jeff, as I shifted about uncomfortably.

There appeared to be no music. When I inquired about it, my eyes were directed toward the ceiling, where I saw a small balcony. In due course it was occupied by three men with balalaikas. I relaxed on my backless bench, ready to enjoy "Grasslands" or one of those wild Russian folk dances.

You won't believe this, but s'help me it's true! The trio played three selections by that great Russian composer, Steven Foster. First "Swanee River," then "Old Black Joe" and a third which I mercifully can't remember.

I suppose this was an attempt to play music pleasing to Americans. It would be so easy to get helpful guidance — if they would only ask for it. It's sad when individuals try so hard to do the right thing.

On the way out of the Metropole we discovered a room labeled "International Bar." We entered and found almost all the tables unoccupied but one, against the wall, where sat a young Russian and his girl friend . . . a pleasant sight, for I have rarely noted any visible evidence of romantic relationships in Moscow. The young man was leaning forward, talking intensely, and from the girl's expression, he was making progress. Between them was a half-empty bottle of champagne, a warming symbol of festivity underway.

The waiter ushered us to that *same table*, indicating that we were to take the two remaining chairs. I was embarrassed and turned to the many other empty tables. But he was adamant. Perhaps this was the custom in Russia and the young couple would be hurt if we rejected them.

It wasn't. The young man had, understandably, taken a lively interest in the dialogue. When we sat down, he rose angrily. Seizing the champagne bottle, he thrust it in my hands, grabbed the girl, and departed.

Both Jeff and I had great respect for that young man. As a matter of fact, we toasted him with his champagne. The waiter didn't seem a bit disturbed by the whole incident. Perhaps his original intention was to concentrate customers, to simplify service. Or maybe it had deeper significance . . . political, religious, or folkloristic. We'll never know.

We had an area labeled "Cocktail Bar" in our hotel, just off the lobby. I sat on a stool, as I might in the States. But instead of the familiar labels against the wall there were about six large bottles, each filled with a colored liquid in brilliant primary hues. It was a difficult decision, in which the girl behind the bar could not help me because she had never tasted any of them . . . whether from observance of rules or self-preservation, I could not determine. I finally selected a deep purple, for which she collected $1.25 before I had tasted it — a wise precaution, born of experience, I'm sure. I sipped it cautiously, briefly, and departed. I can't tell you what it tasted like, because I have no frame of reference. I am sure it was nourishing and wholesome, but I found it depressing.

Again, they mean well. I had some soiled laundry. The hotel had not yet established such an innovation, I was told by the floorlady, when she understood me. But the little woman who cleaned our rooms came back, and after a bit of timid conversation with Jeff, we learned that she was offering to do our washing. We gave her a few shirts, and next day they were back on hangers in our closet, clean but unironed and a frightful mess of wrinkles. She had taken them down to the Volga, perhaps, and slapped them against the rocks to beat out the dirt. We could not wear them but were touched by her gesture, particularly when she refused any payment.

One finds many elderly women doing chores like running elevators. I mentioned to our guide that such a smart new hotel as the Russia should have attractive, nicely uniformed young girls in their elevators, as in many other countries. Her answer was that over *twenty million people* had been killed in World War II. There were tens of thousands of widows without resources who performed such services. I was chastened, and properly embarrassed.

I am sure the toughest aspect of doing business with the Russians is the *correspondence*. Much of it left me with the feeling, "I shot an arrow into the air. It fell to earth, I know not where."

For example, I had hoped to meet a lady, high up in the Soviet hierarchy, who seemed to be in overall charge of Mezh Kniga. I learned she was in Montreal, attending the Soviet exhibit at Expo 70. So I asked Capitol's branch manager in that city to communicate with her and, if possible, arrange a meeting.

It apparently wasn't possible, but our manager did get a request from one of the Russian executives. Mezh Kniga had a large stock of records they had hoped to sell at the Fair. Now, it was closing and the remaining inventory of 50,000 albums would have to be returned to Russia. They would appreciate it if we would buy them and try to sell them in Canada and the U.S.A.

I wrote requesting a list of titles. There was no answer. Then I sent a warehouseman from Toronto to catalog them. It took considerable time, with language difficulties, but when I finally got the list and reviewed it with our sales people, I was able to make a decision. I wrote a letter of acceptance.

Again, no answer. I was annoyed. I called the Russian commercial attache in Washington, whom I knew quite well, and asked him to check it out. He said he would.

And he did. Back came the word that Mezh Kniga had *no* excess inventory in Montreal. They never did have any.

I told my friend that the original request had come from *them*. We had *seen* the inventory, and I had a catalog of the titles, which we had made on the spot.

He said nothing. I realized there was nothing he could say, in his position. We exchanged a few pleasantries and I hung up.

Why? Who knows. Perhaps it developed that such an inventory indicated poor planning, or poor recordings, both reprehensible, and so the subject was dropped.

All I know is that it takes a special kind of businessman to handle Russian foreign affairs, just as it must call for unique personalities in our State Department. And surely, the primary requisite is *patience*!

Someday, I am sure the political tension with Russia will ease, and this will be reflected in business negotiations. Then they will be able to meet and talk like *individuals* rather than as small mouthpieces of a vague, critical behemoth, lurking in the background.

Of course, one must remember that there is *no* competition in Russia, except among people. There is only one record company (what bliss!), one publishing house, one of everything, I suppose. Wits are never sharpened by the business problems that are routine for us. It produces a different race of businessmen, who regard our system with bewilderment and timidity.

For the Soviets' sake and for ours, I hope the bridge of business activities continues to be built, stronger and more secure. For no one wants to fight with his good customers . . . a fact that may ultimately assure continued peace more effectively than atomic submarines.

Of one thing I am sure . . . people's basic emotions are pretty much the same the world over. A common denominator is Disneyland! I've been there endless times with businessmen from far-off countries. Everybody loves it.

The Russians were no exception. When they visited Hollywood, I planned to fly them into Disneyland in a helicopter, landing in the parking lot like Peter Pan. But they informed me that we must go by the long, ugly, freeway route, which is prescribed for them by our government. I got indignant but they said, "Don't worry — we do the same things to your officials!" So many such routines are a product of reciprocity. I understand the Japanese would be happy to eliminate the bother of visas for us — but we insist on it for them. British people don't need visas because they, in turn, do not require any. *Quid pro quo*, the lawyers call it.

The Russians were so delighted with Disneyland they asked me, "Do you suppose we could copy it, on the Black Sea?"

"Of course," I said generously. For all I know they may be building it, taking the funds from their outer-space budget. Disney may sue. If so, I suggest assigning very young lawyers, for they will have a lifetime career.

12

Airports frequently reflect the characteristics of the people. Take Orly, near Paris. It is beautifully designed, and possesses many unique features. Like the public address system. In most airports the scratchy garble that announces the immediate departure of the flight you should be on is almost unintelligible. But at Orly, I am told, the P.A. system comprises endless speakers, about a foot apart in the ceiling, resulting in a young lady's soft, yet readily understood whisper, wherever you might be. I first heard it in the men's room, and found it embarrassingly intimate.

Rio de Janeiro has an airport that is, to put it kindly and avoid international reverberations, limited. But even more interesting than the airport was the road leading to it . . . as I found out early one morning.

I was booked on Lufthansa, leaving Rio for Buenos Aires. Bill Morris, head of our office in Rio, arrived at my hotel at 7:00 A.M. to pick me up. It was raining. I've seen tropical downpours before, but when I stepped out into this I felt the need for an aqualung. We started off, semi-submerged, but had gone only a few blocks when the car gasped, gurgled and died.

Bill, dedicated soul that he is, leaped out into the rain and to my amazement returned shortly with a taxi. He told me he had promised a substantial bonus to the driver upon arrival at the airport — and a smart gambit it proved to be. We splashed on our way.

I must explain about the road to the airport, the only one from Rio at that time. And perhaps now. It was composed, as I recall, of eight lanes, four in each direction. In the center was a dividing area, destined, no doubt, for attractive planting, but now a sodden morass of mud and weeds.

Traffic was heavy, going to the airport. And the lanes were quickly filled. Ultimately we came to a complete stop. I was amazed to see a number of cars ahead, undaunted, were crossing the muddy divider into the lanes going in the opposite direction, where there was little or no traffic.

But traffic in the other lane was forthcoming, headed for the city. The result was inevitable, and apparently this technique was an accepted practice. Eight lanes going to the city met eight lanes coming from it, like galloping knights in pitched battle.

Worse, the area of meeting was low, and completely flooded. I could see cars, standing deeper and deeper in the water, with space in between suggesting complete inundation of at least two lines of combatants. The stalemate was complete and appeared permanent.

I asked Bill why the city didn't repair the road or build a bridge. He said it was really no problem except when it rains.

Our cab driver, however, was not about to be cheated out of his bonus. He shouted something in his native tongue which was no doubt comparable to "I have not yet begun to fight," and spun the wheel as we raced across the open field, ducking around bushes and large rocks. Ultimately we reached a narrow dirt road and followed its twists and turns until we came to the back of the airport. There was a gate, half open, which we went through, crossing the field to the airport building, where I grabbed my bags and headed for Lufthansa.

It was almost an hour after departure time, but the plane had not left. In fact, I was the first passenger to arrive, and I created a mild sensation. When we took off, there was only one other passenger in first class. I was sorry the rain obscured the sight of the road below — an aerial view would have been interesting.

* * *

I shouldn't leave Rio without touching upon the world renowned Carnival. It was sheer coincidence that the affair occurred at the time of my visit. My wife took a dim view of my explanation, as I packed a white tuxedo jacket, but it happens to be true — s'help me! Bill Morris managed to get me a suite in a lush hotel on the famous Copacabana Beach. I learned that all the rooms are booked up years ahead and Bill had wangled this only because the hotel manager, like everyone else, was a frustrated song writer. Bill had agreed to record one of his offerings. I felt a little guilty, wondering what had happened to whoever had reserved the suite eons ago, but I managed to gain control of my emotions and headed for the bar. Here I discovered that an ounce of Kentucky Tavern bourbon costs $2.50, so I decided to sip instead of gulp.

I noticed a chap beside me tossing down drinks at a mad pace. He was an American, a tourist guide traveling with a large and eager group from the states. He told me his sad story:

The touring company had a representative in Rio whose job it was to make hotel bookings and aid in caring for tour groups. For good and sufficient reasons, no doubt, they had recently fired this local agent. And as a parting gesture he had cancelled all of their hotel reservations. This, during Carnival week!

I grew deeply sympathetic as he told a touching story of the large group in a nearby hotel, waiting in the lobby, with baggage piled high around them . . . by now, uneasy, I am sure. I agreed with him that his act in abandoning the group and hiding in a nearby bar was the only path open to him. For to stand there and face them, to tell them that there were not only no rooms at that hotel where they had prepaid reservations . . . and they would soon be ejected from the lobby into the humidity and surging crowds on the sidewalk . . . it was asking too much of any man. There was also a strong element of danger involved. They might fall upon him and dismember him.

After a few more drinks, I offered to extend to a few members of the tour group the solace of my suite, providing I could peer into the lobby next door and pre-select them. I don't know what he thought I had in mind for his response concerned the fact that the youngest woman in the group was in her late fifties, and he suspected that she was lying about her age. It was all very sad. Realizing that he would soon be out of a job and must conserve his resources, I bought him another drink.

Later he grew uneasy, fearful that some members of the group might be reconnoitering. We moved to a more obscure bar on a side street. Here I discovered that Kentucky Tavern bourbon, poured from the bottle did not cost $2.50, but was a mere fifty cents. My friend explained that this was because I was now drinking domestic booze. Seems the Kentucky Tavern folks send to Rio what he described as "flavoring," and the local chaps add alcohol and bottle it with the same labels. As I drank it, I felt vaguely uneasy, but I must confess I could detect no difference.

Later, I offered him the extra bed in my suite, but he declined, feeling that he should leave Rio for some safer spot, like southern Italy, where he had relatives. We parted with pledges of enduring friendship. I never heard from him again. Perhaps they caught him and beat him to death with their hand luggage. I hope not, for he was a nice chap.

* * *

One fast note on the Carnival, for those who have not experienced such a mass orgy. The population of the town and its environs appear in costume and go leaping about the streets, banging on strange bongos and shouting mystic chants. I was told not to mingle, for they greet foreigners with cries of gay camaraderie and embraces, that leave one breathless, and sometimes walletless.

The opening night I was escorted through a frightening crush of wildly costumed natives to a huge old frame building, which was re-

101

served for the aristo'cracy. We sat at a small table, surrounded by a sea of even smaller tables, occupied by innumerable people and their friends who stood behind them, leaning on their shoulders. In the center of some tables stood scantily clad girls, writhing to the rhythms of a variety of bands. Our table did not come so equipped, but I was gratified when an exceedingly well-endowed young lady leaped upon the next table and began shaking among other things, her tassels. I viewed the scene from an interesting perspective and later found that this girl was apparently the *pièce de résistance* of the entire orgy, for her picture appeared on the cover of a local magazine similar to *Life*. In the right-hand corner my shoulder and left elbow are prominently displayed, clothed in a wrinkled, soiled and sweat-soaked white tuxedo jacket.

* * *

Before I left Rio, Bill Morris took me to his vacation home, high in the mountains near Rio. He had a lovely retreat, and I was grateful to escape the tropical heat as we sat on the patio and sipped cold drinks.

I was surprised to see lots of native toads hopping about. I've seen a good share of toads in my time, but these were tremendous. One of them hopped over next to me and eyed me speculatively. Bill said not to be concerned — they were harmless, and actually controlled insect growth. That was apparent, for this toad had an amazingly large grasshopper in his mouth, pinioned by a leg. The toad, ignoring the desperate struggle for life under his nose, munched contentedly on the leg, a bit at a time, bringing the large green body closer for the ultimate *coup de grâce*.

Bill apparently sensed that I found the situation something less than entertaining, for he calmly extracted the grasshopper and tossed him into some nearby bushes. The toad remained, staring at me as if contemplating revenge. I had another drink.

While in the hill country, Bill took me to a very impressive estate occupied by a gentleman who held an important position in the government. He was most gracious, and escorted me around the expansive grounds, ultimately leading into a wild, jungle-like area. As we pushed through the undergrowth, I noted that he wore high, laced boots, in contrast to my low and comfortable moccasins. I asked him why he wore such high shoes in a hot and humid climate. My interest in local flora and fauna dissolved when he made a sweeping gesture around him and hissed, "Serpents!"

* * *

My flight to Buenos Aires was uneventful, except for the man across the way. He occupied the aisle seat. Next to him in the choice window seat, was his bass violin. It apparently was a valuable instrument and he told me he had paid for a first-class seat to have it by his side.

In the U.S.A., I do not think such a maneuver is permitted. I remember a story Pat Barry, my sister-in-law, tells of buying two seats from San Francisco to Los Angeles for herself and a "Mr. Chair." She appeared just as they were closing the gate carrying Mr. Chair . . . who was not a cripple, but an antique. She had bought it at a bargain and figured it would be cheaper and quicker to pay a one way fare for it than have it crated and shipped. The chap at the airline muttered objections and quoted rules, but she turned on the charm, usually reserved for the TV cameras, handed him the two tickets, and breezed through and onto the plane. She said she did not insist on extra cocktails for Mr. Chair during flight.

13

As I reread parts of this book, I am forced to one conclusion: I must have had a lot of fun — living, working, loving . . . coping with life's vagaries.

I did, of course, enjoy life and savor its happier moments. For there are times for all of us to laugh and be joyous.

And for all of us, there are times to cry.

As a young man I read Kipling's famous poem "If," which was classified in the index as "Inspirational." I remember those two lines:

> If you can meet with triumph and disaster
> And treat those two imposters just the same.

It goes on, as you no doubt recall, to conclude "You'll be a man, my son." Personally, I always felt you'd be an idiot. For who is so foolish as to control laughter when happiness prevails? And who is so insensitive to withhold tears when sorrow surrounds every waking hour?

For almost ten years, during the thirties, I faced a situation much more tragic than the Depression. Six months after Doris and I were married, she was diagnosed as having tuberculosis in both lungs. And she was in the hospital for most of the ten long years to follow.

Today the terrible inroads of that dread disease could be easily controlled and conquered with injections and pills. But at that time there was no way of attacking the waxy coating of the TB bacillus. Poor darling, she went through the endless agonies of having all her ribs removed on one side — a surgical horror done in stages, called a thoracoplasty, which was supposed to collapse the lung and enable the cavities to heal.

She was a registered nurse, and had no illusions about her chances of survival. This made it difficult to create conversation when I visited her at the hospital, twice a day, through that endless period. For what can two young people talk about when there is no future for them? There can be no cheerful chitchat about a better apartment, having babies, the plans, hopes and dreams that make life so worth the living.

And, of course, Doris thought about me . . . wondering whether I was eating properly on our limited budget . . . and, I am sure, always the unspoken question concerning a healthy young man's sex urges, and where they might lead him. I had remained celibate through the whole ordeal, always feeling that my deprivations could not be compared with her constant suffering. But I never discussed such matters with her. Perhaps she wouldn't have believed me.

I mustn't dwell on this situation, because I'm sure it makes morbid reading, but one incident comes to me like a thrust of pain in a wound long healed. One bright Sunday I visited the hospital and found her sobbing uncontrollably. She had been listening to the radio and heard a new song . . . a lovely melody, but such a cruel lyric, that finished:

> Why should you cling
> To some faded thing
> That used to be?
> Take care of yourself
> Don't worry about me.

I knew that I simply must find some "occupational therapy" to intrigue Doris' active mind. Both of us liked creative writing, and after a little research on available markets, I came up with the idea of writing stories of the *"True Confessions"* type. There were so many of these magazines that if you got one rejection you could keep mailing the story out, with the hope of ultimate acceptance.

First, we read a good many of them, and developed a formula, which was like this:

Girl meets boy. For about eighteen double-spaced pages, life is ecstatic. Then the next three pages are devoted to the seduction. Today such events are chronicled up to the bedroom, on the bed, then through every thrust to ultimate ejaculation. But in those days we used asterisks. Like this:

> "John, you mustn't!"
> "But darling . . . don't you see . . . it's *got* to be."
> He pulled me into his arms, lips crushed against mine. There was no turning back, I knew. Because I wanted him as he wanted me — eagerly, desperately.
>
> * * * * * * *
>
> When I awoke, I reached over for his hand. He was not there. I sat bolt-upright in bed.

"John," I called. But there was no answer. There never would be any answer.

Following our formula, from then on, all hell breaks loose. She gets pregnant, of course — no pills in those days. And he turns out to be a Grade-A Bastard — they always do. She sinks deeper and deeper into despair, until the last paragraph, when we leave her, a lonely and ruined woman. Thus a strong moral tone is maintained, following a most titillating series of events.

The story was always basically the same; only the setting and characters differed. Doctor and nurse — boss and secretary — pilot and stewardess — on it went. I must say the plots were ingenious. Take the one we wrote involving a man and wife who had long wanted a child. While on a sales trip he was tested at a hospital and found to be sterile. But when he arrived home he was greeted by a happy wife, glowing with good news. You guessed it. She was pregnant.

I was told an actual story recently that almost drove me back to the typewriter. Boss and secretary. Both married with children. Seduction. Both agree life is intolerable apart and they must run away together. They plan to notify their mates at exactly the same moment on a Friday evening, then meet at a far-off motel for the beginning of a glorious life together. He goes through with the bargain. The children stand, bewildered and frightened. His wife weeps and curses him. When you go, she says, remember there can be no returning. He leaves.

He waits at the motel. His lady friend does not arrive. Late that evening he calls her house. In guarded tones she tells him she could *not* go through with it . . . her husband had been so sweet, having dinner all ready, when she was late. And how *could* the children get along without both parents?

If I wrote the story, I'd put the girl in the motel and have the man weasel out. Women like to read about other women suffering, due to the miserable men in their lives.

One of the most provocative plot-stimulators was given to me by a friend, Dom Lamonica, who was taking a short-story course at Columbia. The assignment was to write a story about this: "She lied to him to make his dying hours happy, and he didn't die."

Our first confession story sold for $125 to *True Confessions* magazine. The editor, Beatrice Lubitz, asked for more and paid up to $175 for a great many that followed — a fortune, during the Depression. More important, Doris was thrilled, and I would find her sitting up in her hospital bed, eyes shining, ready to tell me about a new twist or a new plot she had developed from conversation with the nurses. At last we had something to talk about, something to anticipate.

While Doris was in the hospital I lived in a small hotel room. It had one window which opened on an areaway, with a red-brick wall, close enough to touch, comprising the vista. This was before the advent of air conditioning and on a hot summer day in Manhattan my room seemed unbearable. But it cost only seven dollars a week in those days of depression, and even that was somewhat more than I could afford.

When I wasn't visiting my wife in the hospital, or scratching out a living, or helping with True Confessions, I was writing the Great American Novel, occupational therapy of all neophyte writers. As I look back, I recall that my story concerned the degeneration of a well-educated and talented young man who married a sleazy girl. She remained at her low level, unaffected by him, and he went down, down, down ... to a final dissolute state, when he could no longer support her, and she kept him.

Then I created a second girl for the sole purpose of seeing him through another's eyes, a girl who had loved and lost him. Not too long ago, I unearthed the old manuscript and realized one of its many flaws. My story was not about the man and his wife, and their relationship. It was about the *other girl*, created merely as a point of observation. She had taken over; her hopes, fears, dreams and despair dominated the story. And that was not the way I planned it!

But in the summer's heat I would grind away at my manuscript, stripped to my shorts and glistening with sweat. When I would reach an impasse in plot or phrasing, I'd pull on my clothes and walk the streets in frustration.

I knew I wasn't writing very much, or very well. How could I, stuck in that Black Hole of Lexington Avenue, with no air, no comforts ... no inspiration? The summer passed and another after it but my book remained unfinished.

Then I ran across a new book, just published, that I found magnificent. The characters were truly alive, the dialogue crackled with reality, as the story moved toward its inescapable climax. In a short time it reached the top of the best-seller list.

I began to read articles about the author, and his life. Seems he had written this book in a small hotel room. It was in Manhattan, and the same summer when I was trying to write. In fact it was the *same hotel*, The Pickwick Arms, which still may be there. Perhaps he was up the hall from me.

The writer? It was John Steinbeck. His book? "The Grapes of Wrath."

I have never been able to confirm this story. But I have always remembered it. It proves so eloquently that if you've got the talent and the *guts*, you can write *anywhere* — with no need for whimpered excuses. I remember a poem, read in a high school textbook. I can't recall who wrote it but some of the lines fitted me:

Old Homer owned no inch of ground
But sang, and passed the hat around
And eased the pressure of his grief
With a stub of pencil, and a leaf.

For what avails a sea of ink
For he who has no thoughts to think?

*   *   *

As a final act in my personal tragedy, I developed fluid on my lung, a grim harbinger of tuberculosis. I had to tell Doris because the doctor insisted I go to the Trudeau Sanitarium at Saranac Lake, over a hundred miles away, and *not worry about anything*. There was no conversation between us after I told her. Just hopeless, helpless tears.

At Saranac, I was put to bed for prolonged and prone rest. The therapy at that time was to open all the windows, reducing the temperature to well below zero in that mid-winter mountain climate. Then an hour later, I would slowly emerge from the covers as the nurse would close all windows and heat the room until you would sweat. Nobody ever explained to me why this was a good idea. They just did it. I learned later that there was a big TB sanitarium in California at Monrovia where patients were made to sit in the sun. Puzzling.

They had what were called "up patients" who, when they became vertical, would go around visiting new patients to cheer them. A young lady bounced into my room and asked how I felt.

"Fine," I said. "I don't really have TB. It's just that there was some fluid on my lung and the doctor didn't want to take any chances."

She laughed. "They all say that at first. But they wind up out there," she gestured toward the window.

I looked out. It was a graveyard.

"We call it Dr. Trudeau's garden," she quipped and moved on to cheer up the next patient.

Years later, when the TB plague was completely controllable through medication, The American Management Association bought the whole Trudeau Sanitarium and made a college out of it. Ironically I attended a training course for executives up there, again in mid-winter. How wonderful that the medical services were no longer needed, and the place could be converted to such a purpose.

I can't resist, at this point, telling one brief story about this management course. Here we were — several hundred middle-aged executives — all holed up in this remote bastion — no booze, no girls, nothing but continuous study on How To Be A Better Executive.

But every night they ran movies, and we all attended. The night

109

before we left it was "Cat On a Hot Tin Roof." You may remember . . . early in the picture there is a scene showing Elizabeth Taylor dressing. She is obviously suffering from her husband's neglect of his marital responsibilities, as she slowly — very slowly — pulls on one stocking. Then she raises her leg high and oh-so-slowly pulls on the other slinky silky stocking. (You could hear a cigar ash drop in the auditorium at this point.)

When the scene was finished, great cheers went up. "Run it again," we shouted. The projectionist obliged, and we got a second view of Miss Taylor's endowments. It was repeated again after that. I don't believe we ever got to see the entire picture. Maybe it got even better.

I suppose most of the "students" had lurid dreams that night. I'm afraid I didn't. I was haunted by memories of the place. One brief week after I had been sent there for bed rest, the head nurse came in and told me my wife was dead.

Then she dropped on her knees and said, "Let us pray." I wasn't much good at that sort of thing but I did my best.

I read a poem recently, written by an old lady of 79, Rose Fine, who has since died.

> God, since thou art unknown
> I doubt even thee.
> But then there is the sun,
> And the great sea.
> God, I'm not one of those
> Blinded by belief.
> But who else can tinge a rose
> Or make a leaf?
> Whenever the rain,
> Sweet and clear
> At my window taps
> My lips move, so my soul can hear,
> Who knows . . . perhaps.

All this talk about heaven . . . where we are reunited with our loved ones. What will I do with two wives . . . Doris and Priscilla. I know them well . . . neither would share me with the other, not even for one brief eon. And I love them both. Problems, even up there.

14

A sad aspect of the men who travel around the world on an expense account is that most of them are not young. In fact, in some, like me, the flush of youth has faded and there is a general droop and sag, the result of flying too many miles, first class, and sitting too many hours in long meetings which are followed by gastronomical orgies in which one must actively participate to show appreciation.

One time in Barcelona I was being entertained at a large and lavish restaurant which, naturally enough, featured Spanish food. I had, in a moment of bravura, stated that I spoke "some" Spanish. I have used this gambit in many countries, hoping that during business negotiations it would have a tendency to limit "asides" in native tongues like, "We've got this bastard on the rack — let's give the wheel a few turns and see if he screams."

In Japan, of course, they knew I spoke a language of traveling men known as Geisha Japanese, and they need only to avoid phrases like "You are very beautiful — what are you doing after the tea-pouring ceremony?"

In fairness, I did speak *some* Spanish. In my high school days, the ruling hierarchy had decreed that students could not graduate without two years of a foreign language. Discreet inquiries among my peers revealed that Spanish was far easier than French, German or Latin. Perhaps it was. Anyhow, I was exposed to it for two years, and the only pleasure extracted was getting acquainted with *Don Quixote*, I being a bit of a windmill tilter myself.

But the actual application of my Spanish has been limited to conjugating a few verbs with Flamenco dancers. So when my host handed me the elaborate menu, I was nonplussed to discover it was in Spanish. But I carried on bravely, pretending to study the various items and making

111

little clucking noises of approval as I progressed. This procedure ultimately wore out the patience of my host, and he placed his own order, which involved considerable conversation and gestures, and was impressive.

Then it was my turn. And from my old mouldering text book in Spanish II, floated the magic words.

"*Los mismos!*" I said, with a gesture far more sweeping than any used at the table.

I knew I had scored heavily. "*Los mismos*," for those among my readers who lack the advantages of my educational background, means "the same." I had thus given sweeping approval to my host as a gourmet, and in his native tongue. Everyone smiled and nodded approval.

I did not savor my triumph very long, however. For the food began to arrive ... strange and squirmy. My first dish was quite obviously pickled spiders, a larger species than I had seen, and perhaps with more legs. My host popped them into his mouth individually, and I had no choice but to follow. Later, discreet inquiries revealed that they were baby octopi, apparently plucked from their mother's bosom at a very tender age. I won't say they were tasty, but I did manage to control rumblings of regurgitation.

The entree comprised bicycle tires, but in cross slices and stewed in an appropriate lubricant. While the rubbery resilience remained, the flavor had been somewhat enhanced and it required only vigorous mastication and a mind free from prejudice to swallow each morsel. Later I learned that apparently Mother Octopus had been captured with her babies, and her large and long tentacles sliced up.

Judging by the dishes that followed I am sure nothing had been wasted from the creature, who, no doubt, participated in the entire meal, except perhaps the dessert. It was a memorable, and I am sure expensive, meal.

* * *

But I got a bit off the track. I was talking about businessmen who are world travelers being older and tiring more easily. In my case, I found great solace and comfort in having an occasional massage. I don't mean the kind you get at the Athletic Club, administered by a sweating male sadist who appears on your monthly bill under "Physiotherapy." Or the type in Nordic countries where they grill you over a slow fire, roll you in the snow, then beat you with bundles of sticks. There is only one place in the world to get a massage, and that is *Japan*.

My first massage was in a small country hotel, deep in the Japanese highlands. I was on the last leg of my first round-the-world trip, arranged and booked by Capitol's president, Glenn Wallichs, who approved my expense account. Glenn no doubt reasoned that if he gave me extra time in any place I would get into trouble, so I was limited to adequate hours for travel, business, sleeping, shaving and such. In less than three weeks' time I touched at London, Paris, Barcelona, Milan, Cologne, Vienna, Athens, Istanbul, Bangkok, Singapore, and Tokyo. This schedule of course included over 25,000 miles of flying time, endless meetings with business associates, and frequent elaborate meals and entertainment, for our branch managers were most hospitable.

When I finished the last meeting in Tokyo I was in a state of physical and gastronomical exhaustion. My friend and colleague Warren Birkenhead, who represented us in Japan, pushed me in his little car and drove far, far away. We ultimately stopped before a small Japanese inn, high in the mountains. Here he led me by the hand to a charming room overlooking a lovely garden, where I disrobed, put on a soft voluminous kimono and sat on a pillow. He left me and closed the door.

A light rain was falling . . . just a gentle pitter-patter on the rooftop. I looked out at the garden and the hills beyond, with the faint form of Fuji just visible.

Three hours later I was still sitting there. Never have I felt more relaxed. Dunn, the galloping executive, who scheduled every hour and analyzed its productivity, was out for the count.

There was a gentle tap at my door. In came a little Japanese doll who had apparently escaped from her glass display case. She dropped to her knees, bowed low, and proceeded to give me a massage. No, it wasn't one of those sexy affairs you've heard about. My robe remained on as I stretched out prone on a flowered mattress. Her fingers flowed over me like a gentle rivulet . . . sheer, sensuous poetry.

Then I began to sing, softly. Go ahead — laugh. I always sing when I'm happy! It just comes out, like cats purr.

She corrected my words and phrasing of "Sakura," a song about cherry blossoms, and giggled at my blending of Japanese with Brooklynese. Soon we were singing together.

She was with me for almost two hours. When she had finished, she took my hand and led me to an adjoining suite, where I found Warren, stretched out in the semi-buff and in the process of being thumped and chopped by a plump elderly lady of grim visage. He looked up at my doll and crudely commented, "You lucky bastard." The girl smiled, bowed to both of us and stepped out of my life.

For a long time I ambled around in my kimono with a Mona Lisa-like smile. The rain had stopped, and with it every ache, every muddled thought, every concern for the past or future. Many times since I've wished that I could recapture that mood and feeling. But I know, of course, that such ephemeral experiences return again only as warming memories.

* * *

I have had many massages since, none quite so idyllic, but relaxing enough. It is quite legitimate to have a massage girl come to your room in any Japanese hotel. Personally, I always found this activity possessed an illicit aura . . . which perhaps I savored.

But requesting a massage girl from your hotel room in Tokyo is strictly a Russian roulette procedure. You phone downstairs and wait. Soon there is a gentle tap-tap-tap at your door and in she slips . . . an elderly muscular matron who can leave you bruised and aching, or perhaps a petite charmer that conducts her activities with the finesse of Maestro Osawa with the Tokyo Symphony. She assists you in having a hot tub bath, and when you collapse on the bed, with a towel spread across your midriff, she starts to work. Later, when she slips away in the night, you are asleep — with a smile on your face — before the door closes.

* * *

The cutest massage girl I ever encountered was at the stately Okura, one of Tokyo's finest hotels. She spoke a little English, which I discovered when I was flat on my face and she was standing in front of me, kneading the area where most men have shoulder muscles. Fearful of being pitched off the bed, I groped for the bedpost to hang on. She suddenly stopped and I discovered to my chagrin that I was clutching her legs, slightly above the ankles. She stepped back and looked at me with an air of polite inquiry.

"You have massage license?" she asked.

Later, when flat on my back with a small towel across the strategic area, she was pulling on my toes — a routine that must be taught by the Chief Inquisitor at the massage academy, for they all do it, producing a snapping sound that suggests dislocation. As I twisted and turned, the towel slipped, exposing, under the bright light, my limitations.

With the dignity of a Philadelphia matron, she stopped, picked up the towel and replaced it.

"You catch cold," she said.

* * *

Another type of massage which has merit, on occasion, is the type of treatment wherein you descend to a subbasement in the hotel, where you are escorted to a small cubicle containing a sunken tub, a pail, a bench, a table, and a girl. The one I drew was charming, as she stood there in tight white shorts and a bra made from the trimmings, no doubt. The door was closed but it contained a small window, so Mamma-San could peek in at intervals to keep everything legit. I had been coaxed out of my shorts, so was slumping before this lovely lady wearing nothing but a look of embarrassment. She smiled in a most friendly fashion as I looked into her shining eyes.

One thing you learn quickly in Japan is that you never — *never* — place your unwashed torso into a tub of clean, hot water. There is a standard procedure, which she followed. She filled a bucket with water, twirled a cake of soap in it for a few moments, then sopped up some with a woolly cloth. She then soaped me from head to foot, with all stops in between. And if this process sounds sexy or titillating, let me assure you that it encompassed all the romantic charm of being processed at your local car-wash.

Little did I know that behind her big, black beautiful eyes was a mind of a Marquis de Sade. For when I was heavily soaped, she emptied the bucket, washed it out, and dipped out a pail of liquid fire from the tub. With a quick gesture she flung it at an area sometimes described as the "family jewels."

My scream of pain was echoed by the obbligato of her high-pitched giggle.

Then she scalded the rest of my anatomy to match, and nudged me into the tub for a long parboiling before the massage.

When she was ready for the massage I was in such a flabby stupor that I had to be helped up on the table. The actual manipulations that followed were a matter of complete indifference to me. I was asleep.

Massages are also available at endless institutions throughout Tokyo. I understand that there are some services of a more personal nature, which one might regard as a sub-rosa activity, but which are emblazoned on neon signs outside. I can't read Japanese, so couldn't check it out. One time I did encounter an aspiring ballerina who danced to a tape recording of "Swan Lake" — this, on my spine, while her toes manipulated my vertebrae. I have never been able to hear the melody since without twitching.

* * *

I could go on talking about massage girls for endless pages, but I know how boring this could be to Americans who enjoy cold showers and therefore cannot "relate." But I must tell you about No. 19.

I had been negotiating an involved and sticky contract with Toshiba, concerning our partnership. This deal was particularly difficult because it involved the U.S., U.K., and Japan — where ultimate approval had to be obtained from the government. And I had been working all day through an interpreter, a tiring and slow procedure.

That night I staggered back to the Hilton and immediately sat down in my room to get on paper the complexities of the day while my little mind still retained them. I wanted to phone Bill Stanford, head of EMI's International Division, in London, and get his thoughts on the happenings, but due to the drastic time difference I could not place the call until 1:00 A.M.

It was close to 10:00 P.M. I had finished my reports, had a light supper in my room and was tired. But I had almost three hours before the London call. I decided to have a massage. And from the depths of the hotel's basement where the girls are sequestered until needed, came No. 19 — the only name I ever knew her by in the years following.

No. 19 was quietly businesslike about the whole process. She was not beautiful, but neat and professional looking. In no time she was kneading and pounding with painful but pleasant vigor. She spoke practically no English, so my mind reverted to the phone call I must make.

Then she started to sing. Not one of those vague, lovely Japanese melodies, but, of all things, American operetta . . . "Lover Come Back to Me" from "New Moon."

As an operetta buff, I go back to the original version of "The Student Prince," in New York about 1925, when the lyric of the marching song, "Come boys, let's all be gay boys," didn't have today's implications. I saw it with a vivacious dark-eyed beauty named Mary Taylor while attending high school. She was the belle of the school, and the steady date of the football captain, who outranked me, as editor of the school paper and base viol player in the orchestra. But she was a music lover, and it was a memorable night when we squeezed together in the subway, headed for the bright lights of Broadway. It was a thrilling evening in every respect, and later, as we walked up the dark street to her home singing "Deep in My Heart," I felt she must now be aware that there were finer things in life than shouting signals to a bunch of sweating oafs on a football field. But she disappeared in the doorway of her brownstone front with an airy wave of her lovely hand . . . not even the smallest dividend for my investment of $6.60 for the two tickets. In the following week I could only afford a nickel chocolate bar for lunch, and was inclined to be morose.

Back to No. 19. It seems that for a long time she had been a music major at some school in Tokyo. Instead of singing songs about cherry blossoms she sang operetta — almost every one known to Broadway. She had a lovely voice, but as she knew very little English, she sang the words by rote, creating the sounds but not understanding them. Her "Wover come black to me" was most charming and quite contemporary in its philosophy.

Now, while I am sure there are varying opinions on the subject, I also sing. And I also know every operetta, from the opening chorus, when the peasants come leaping on the stage, to the last act, when the boy and girl, reunited, cling together nose to nose, screaming love songs. Having thumped a banjo for years, I am also familiar with chords and can vocalize saccharine harmony notes with tender inflections.

So I joined No. 19 in song, and sweet harmony echoed through the room as she kneaded my muscles. We began with several arias from "The Desert Song" and continued through almost the complete score of "The Vagabond King." I can still feel the bruises from her rhythmic thumping to the "Song of the Vagabonds": "Sons of toil and danger, will you serve a stranger, and bow down to Burgundy!"

Then the phone rang, loud and jangling during our tender reprise of "The Indian Love Call" from "Rose Marie." Clinging to my towel, I answered it. What friend could be calling me so late?

It wasn't a friend. It was the Assistant Manager from the lobby below. His tone lacked warmth and respect as he advised me that it was against the rules to have a party in one's room so late. Non-music lovers among the nearby guests were objecting.

I glanced at my watch. It was close to 2:00 A.M. No. 19 departed in a hurry, looking worried and embarrassed, as I placed the call to London.

In the years that followed, No. 19 and I expanded our repertoire considerably. We got to be good friends, and one time I invited her to a nearby restaurant called the Alte Libre, noted for its music, supplied by talented students and teachers from Tokyo's music schools. (I took Warren Birkenhead along to avoid implications.) No. 19 appeared in formal kimono, shy, silent, and expressionless, even when fellow students greeted her.

I was hailed by some of my brother's enthusiastic friends . . . he is a movie cameraman and had done several projects for the Osaka Fair. I introduced Warren, then stopped, feeling very foolish. For how could I say, "May I present No. 19?"

My career in the Orient came to a close and I may never again go to Tokyo. So in parting may I raise a cup of hot sake to a fine singer and a charming lady . . . to you, No. 19!

15

I suppose it was two years before I emotionally adjusted to the death of my first wife, Doris. The memory of her beauty, her love — her endless pain and tragic death — will always be with me. But when one is in one's mid-thirties, life has a way of gradually softening the shadows of sadness. For you must go on living and, I am sure, loving.

I had a good job, a nice apartment, and a growing urge. But I also had a lot of things that needed updating after a decade of being out of circulation.

Had I been a used car, recently placed back on the lot, the repairs and refinishing would be obvious. Grind the valves, new plugs, replace worn-out battery with a new one (high powered!). And of course new whitewalls and a paint job in some brighter color. I would not get many miles to the gallon, but might catch an occasional eye, and would be functional.

I knew that some of the ingredients for my rehabilitation were intangible. Others were quite apparent . . . a good place to begin.

My dancing obviously needed close attention, for there had been many developments in that area since a fellow high school student had patiently taught me all he knew — comprising sort of a hopping step, and on every third hop you grabbed the girl close, for a moment. I suspect it was all a product of his own ingenuity, but found it offered certain basic advantages, once your partner got over the initial shock and realized your maneuvers were rhythmic, not rapacious.

But now there were a lot of Latin steps. And I had been trapped on a few occasions, when after having waited a considerable period for a fox trot of exactly the right tempo to fit my limitations, I found myself standing stark on the floor as the orchestra burst into a Conga or Samba, with everybody leaping joyously about. Except me and my date, whose smile of delight at the first smack of the bongo had quickly frozen into one of polite resignation.

Arthur Murray had run a good deal of advertising about wallflowers blossoming into a torrid lovelife through adroit application of his Basic Step. I went to their midtown studios for a free analysis, where I was introduced to a ravishing blonde in a red evening gown, who responded to my three hops and a grab with flattering phrases. It seems that I was gifted with a natural rhythm and grace, coupled with considerable originality. All I needed was their brush-up course, to pick up some of the newer steps. In a warm glow of anticipation, I wrote my check and made my initial appointment.

Then things changed. The lady in red was not available for my first lesson. I was introduced to a tall, substantially built woman, with an attitude suggesting that we were about to engage in an athletic contest, in which she had the obvious edge.

But the worst part of the episode was when I was taken into a room, the walls of which were *lined with mirrors*. There I saw myself at angles never before visible. My shoulders were round. I seemed to possess an unnatural slump. And the jacket sagged in the back, instead of, for better or worse, fitting my form. It was all pretty shocking.

It's funny, the illusions we have about ourselves. I had begun to fancy myself as a bit of a Rex Harrison, with perhaps a Cary Grantish touch, but here was nothing but a lumpy Lloyd reflected at me from every awful angle.

I never went back for another lesson, figuring that if I was going to edge my way into the promised torrid love life, I would have to depend on salesmanship and booze.

* * *

I must tell a similar Pygmalion story that had a happier ending. I had recently been hired by McGraw-Hill as an editorial assistant. After a period, during which I kept mislaying important memos and writing notes to editors in an undecipherable scrawl, my several bosses conferred and decided to get me a secretary.

In my position, clinging to the bottom rung of the ladder, I was not granted any selectivity. The personnel department reached down deep in the barrel and sent me a specimen designed to offer no distraction from work. I shall call her Miss Fitz.

Miss Fitz lacked almost every one of the goodies that men lust after. One glance convinced me that my bosom was more ample than hers. Her legs were thin and straight — the kind that don't fill out stockings and leave morbid, little wrinkles. And her clothes draped on her like they had been hung on a hook. But she wore a pleasant smile, and she was the first secretary I had ever "owned." I was grateful.

As the months went by, Miss Fitz became invaluable. She put things in places where she could find them, hit the right keys on the typewriter, and always answered the phone with a cheerful, "Mr. Dunn's office." I had no office — just a desk next to hers out in the open with the other peasants. But it warmed my heart to hear her.

We were working late one evening when she confided in me. She had no boy friends. She had employed every gambit, but no discernible response was ever forthcoming. Even the milkman pushed the bill under her door, instead of coming in, as he did in the other apartments. What *could* she do?

By this time, if I may say so, I had developed a small reputation as a merchandiser. I had started my business life as a commercial artist, and as I turned to copywriting had developed some latent sense of how and where to sell things.

I became intrigued with Miss Fitz's problem. Because it suddenly struck me that here was a routine merchandising problem. First — and most vital in this case — the product must be repackaged. Then the market must be located where this product had the best chance of selling.

I cautiously suggested a procedure. She, desperate soul, urged that we start immediately.

The new packaging aspect was perhaps the most interesting. I was certainly not qualified in such areas, but I had a friend who was. He was a Frenchman and a portrait photographer — Joe Capitaine. I bought Joe a lunch and sold him on the challenge. Joe, who spent most of his business hours posing really beautiful ladies, was intrigued by this switch.

A few weeks later the change in Miss Fitz was noticeable and startling. Joe had shown her how to use makeup to emphasize her best features and subordinate "problem areas." He had taken "before and after" pictures that were truly amazing. Her high forehead receded, her sallow complexion blossomed and I had never before realized that her eyes were deep and lustrous.

Also, in some unaccountable way, her bosom had developed an intriguing projection. And her clothes were colorful and seemed to emphasize curves never before apparent.

With all this, came a vivaciousness born of self-confidence. She began to attract attention from outside our two-desk periphery, which first pleased me and then got to be a nuisance.

When it came time to develop a marketing plan for the new product, I found out it really wasn't required. No, I didn't fall in love with her. But somebody else did. And when she resigned to take a better job, with marriage on the horizon, I extended my hand to congratulate her. Instead, she gave me a kiss — not the sort of peck one might expect, but a real grabber. Then she said, "Thank you," in a new husky, sexy voice she had developed, and walked out of my life to live, I am sure, happily ever after.

* * *

I feel an urge to tell you about the Hotel 14, so called because its address was 14 East 60th, right next to the Copacabana night club, famed for its elaborate shows and beautiful chorus line.

The "14" was a very old, quaint hotel, distinguished by the fact that it had a large, handsome bar called the Burgundy Room. Somehow this spot became a headquarters for a group of unmarried men in their middle thirties. One unkind and perhaps jilted young lady dubbed the club "The WOWs," which she explained stood for "Worn Out Wolves." I hardly think her limited research justified the title, but the name stuck and spread around town. Soon the members were rather proud of it.

The WOWs were a motley group of widowers, divorced men, and other assorted outcasts, bound together by our lack of home ties, our fondness for drinking, and our appreciation of pretty girls.

For the Copa girls' chorus was right next door. And during intermission, and after shows, some of the girls would slip through the passage connecting the two buildings in the basements, and join the conviviality. They were all beautiful, zany, and fun. I do not believe that any of our eager crew were able to date one of the glamorous creatures, but we bought them drinks happily and took what one of our chaps called a "paternal interest" in them. If true, my feelings verged on the incestuous.

As the club's reputation spread, other young ladies would appear . . . curious, or perhaps hoping to find "Mr. Right." A sad shopping center, I'm afraid. But the bar and restaurant were presided over by a charming hostess known only as "Eleanor." It was against the law to introduce people at such an institution, so she avoided complications by saying "Hello, Lloyd! You remember Janice, don't you?" I always did.

The bartender, Mack, was an affable and beloved gentleman. He loaned money, gave advice to the lovelorn, and joined in the conversation whenever it interested him. Occasionally when I appeared to be making headway with some charmer, he would shake his head negatively — she was not for me. And he was usually right. He is now retired, and we still exchange Christmas cards.

Only one girl lived at the hotel — Sophie Goode. She was a fashion designer — tall, slender, most attractive, and with a devastating sense of humor. Whenever things got dull in the Burgundy Room, we'd try to intrigue Sophie down from her apartment, and take turns propositioning her. Nobody ever got to first base, because, as she explained, she was a lady of unassailable virtue, and besides we were a bunch of no-good bums, unworthy of her favors. She was right, of course.

Came the day when Sophie announced she was returning to her native city in Canada, to be married to a worthy chap, I am sure. I wonder if she ever got the cable we sent her . . . "LOCAL BOY MAKES GOODE."

* * *

The summer headquarters for the WOWs was an old wooden hotel, located on the Jersey shore. It was called the Allaire — pronounced, I was told, "I'll-lay-her."

My first visit there was with Bill Stuart, a McGraw-Hill editor who became a widower at almost the same time I did. About a year later, we both wound up in the WOWs and decided to share a room at the Allaire and see if it lived up to its reputation.

Our room was uninspiring and lacked an ocean-front view, but the place was booked solid and we were glad to get in. We wandered down to the beach to see what we could see.

"Smorgasbord!" exclaimed Bill, with the enthusiasm of the first successful gold-panner at Sutter's Creek. We stood there for quite a while, gazing at an endless display of assorted limbs extending from lovely ladies in scanty bathing attire.

The place showed great promise of living up to its billing. But Bill and I immediately disagreed on the most productive modus operandi. I was all for playing the field and extracting as many phone numbers as possible, to last us through the long cold winter nights in Manhattan. "Plan your work and work your plan," I told him, using an old sales cliché.

But he was caught up in the euphoria of the situation, and planned to grab off the most desirable damsel and quickly develop a warm — and very close — relationship. I told him the story about the grasshopper and the ants, but he would have none of it.

As the days — and nights — passed, Bill proved to have more basic stamina than I, perhaps because he didn't spread himself so thin. He used to stagger into our room at the Allaire long after I had hit the sack, exhausted from drinking, dancing, and generally dispensing my charm in the pursuit of happiness.

Our room was illuminated by a bare light bulb in an old floor lamp which had long since lost its shade. I turned it off when I went to bed, but when Bill tottered in he usually tripped over my bed, and once jammed his arm through the window, seeking the light switch. It was all pretty messy, and so I left the light on thereafter.

But this one night the glaring bulb seemed to burn through my closed eyelids . . . perhaps because I had touched too many bases that night. Anyhow, the solution seemed suddenly obvious. I took a large and woolly bath towel and draped it over the bare bulb. It produced a soft glow that was most soothing as I drifted off to sleep.

I awakened rather suddenly. Bill had not yet returned. But *something* was going on.

The place was brilliant under a sweep of flames, gaily dancing across the walls. The room was on fire!

Now who would have thought that the towel would catch fire and flames extend to the old curled wallpaper and assorted gee-gaws?

Never lacking in courage, particularly when facing imminent immolation, I leaped from the bed, wet a bath towel in the sink and began to beat the flames into submission.

It was then that I realized I had gone to bed in the buff — for fragments of flaming wallpaper were dropping on me and appeared in the act of building up a bright future in the pubic hair area.

But I was making headway, capering about like a disheveled dervish, and producing clouds of black smoke, as the flames faded.

There was a great banging on the door. I had somehow aroused my neighbors. Perhaps the black smoke, pouring out under the door and down into the lobby, had stimulated their curiosity. To quote a former associate, "It was a situation that was fast becoming a predicament." I dared not stop beating the flames and go groping in the smoky murk to find my pants before opening the door. And opening the door without even shorts, exposing my anatomy in this Dante-like setting, seemed bad taste.

My dilemma dissolved in the crash of the door as the impatient multitudes poured in, eager to help. Pandemonium prevailed until the smoke got so thick they were all beating each other with assorted garments belonging to our festive wardrobes.

Exit, choking. But the fire was out, and someone had again broken the recently repaired window, so the smoke poured out, aided by the draft from the hall. The place was a mess. I was a mess, as I told my story in the lobby, before a substantial and appreciative audience.

Several hours later, when I was back, tucked into my sooty sheets, Bill ambled in. He had been in another part of town, dancing with his lady love. When I explained what had happened he started to laugh. He laughed so hard he sat on the edge of the bed and held his head. When I told him that most of *his* clothes had been used to flail the flames he burst into louder guffaws. He was that kind of a guy.

I thought the hotel officials would inflict all sorts of legal and financial horrors on me the next morning. But instead, it seems I was the local hero. People I had never seen came up to talk to me. Nobody asked how the fire *started*. They were grateful to me for my principal role in putting it *out*!

* * *

The depression of the 30's faded into the wartime of the 40's. There were many times I felt uncomfortable about not being in the armed forces. Unlike the Viet Nam affair, in the battle against Hitler we all knew what we were fighting for, and relatively few shirked their responsibilities.

I had been too young for World War I, and almost too old for World War II, as 38 was where the draft stopped. I had just reached 37 and was caring for my first wife, who was dying from tuberculosis. I was classified, first, as a "hardship case." Then for a while I was 4-F, due to the fluid in my lung and my close contact with the disease. Finally they summoned me for another "physical."

I remember arriving early at Exposition Hall in Grand Central, that was used for "processing." I had to take off my clothes — every stitch — and was pushed into a huge, vacant room with enough benches to seat the Russian Army. All empty.

It's a funny thing, but selecting a seat in an empty auditorium is difficult — particularly when one doesn't know where the best seat will turn out to be. But I finally put my bare bottom on a board and unfolded my New York Times, which I had clutched to my skin. This action attracted the attention of a nearby gentleman — perhaps a sergeant. He strode over, snatched the paper from my hands, and tossed it into a scrap barrel. No word of rebuke was spoken, but I assumed I committed some serious breach of behavior.

Gradually the room filled. I doubt if you, gentle reader, have ever been in a really large room packed with stark naked male bodies. It was a depressing sight, as everyone looked uneasily about.

I waited and twitched. We all waited and twitched. Some scratched. One or two started up a friendly conversation but were silenced by a bellowing rebuke from the sergeant.

We waited. It was then I realized that doing *absolutely nothing* is the world's hardest work. Try it sometime, with all your clothes off, so you can't even stick your hands in your pockets.

Then came an unintelligible order, and we started on our way. We went through hearing tunnels (watcha say?), heartbeat checks, knee tappings. The test for homosexuality was obviously not prepared by the Mayo brothers. Some underling snarled, "D'like girls?" in a tone that suggested either a positive or negative response would get you in trouble. My reply, "Some of them," was not considered clever.

When we arrived at one post, something happened that I will never understand, even granting the old adage, "There's the right way, and the Army way." The long line of men was sweating from a previous jumping and squatting exercise in which I was something less than average in performance. We now approached what looked like a small, quaint Japanese bridge — the kind you'd see over bubbling brooks, and usually painted red. This one, however, was raw dirty wood.

Seems you were supposed to walk to the highest point of the bridge and there, in a glaring spotlight, you bent over as in supplication, and "spread your cheeks" . . . non-facially speaking.

So be it. When my turn came, I stepped forward in a manly fashion and assumed the angle, followed by the prescribed gesture.

But no brisk "OK" was forthcoming. Apparently I was being observed and chatted about, quietly and amiably. I waited like a good soldier, bent over and waiting orders.

Ultimately orders came, but instead of waving me on with the other peasants, I was pulled back down, with a gesture indicating I was to wait.

I waited. There was absolutely nothing to look at but the endless chain of nude, sweating colleagues. I was strategically located to observe them . . . stepping up, bending over, spreading cheeks, hesitating, "OK," moving on. To an incipient proctologist the vista might have held a certain academic interest. To a man of my delicate sensibilities it was monstrously grisly.

But I waited. I waited until the last — forgive me — asshole had been exhibited and departed with its owner.

Then the doctor, or whatever he was, waved me on to join the rest. Never an explanation! No physical rejection for a double hernia, or a prostrate prostate. I was the last man through and was classified 1-A.

It was a rating I carried until the end of the war. I also carried an uneasy feeling that something wasn't quite right in my personal areas. But I'm still functional.

* * *

A few years ago I was in New York, staying at Capitol's suite in the Sherry Netherland. One evening I wandered around the corner for a sentimental journey to our old hunting grounds, the Hotel 14. The Burgundy Room was shuttered and dark. Someone told me later that there had been a murder there and the police had closed it. Again proving that one must never return to burnish cherished memories. Things change. And so do we.

* * *

After a few years at McGraw-Hill I reached the rung of the ladder where I could "accept or reject" secretarial applicants. And my rejector was in high gear. For it was amazing the number of assorted shrews our personnel department weeded out of its secretarial pool for my inspection. They came up, one by one, clutching in their hands a company document certifying to their shorthand and typing abilities and other non-essential details.

In those days, McGraw-Hill was located in what became known as the Pistachio Building. The McGraws felt that by erecting this high and handsome green structure in such a dubious location, the whole neighborhood would be inspired to throw out the Flea Circus, the porno movie houses, persistent sidewalk salesmen, and other assorted crud. Unfortunately this never happened. And I hear they are now happily ensconced on the Avenue of the Americas, which was already successfully uplifted by Time-Life, CBS, RCA and other giants of industry.

In desperation I wrote an ad of my own for insertion in the Sunday *Times*. It was friendly, informal, and suggested — I hoped — to some pretty girl that I would be a charming chap to work for. There were quite a number of replies, and selecting those that were most literate, I set aside an afternoon for interviewing.

The desk where I worked was out in an open area known as the bullpen. I had gained some degree of exclusivity by creating a cubicle with filing cabinets and old bookcases, but it was not the most impressive setup for interviews. Fortunately my boss, Bill Beard, was out of town, and he had the largest, fanciest office on the floor. So, ignoring the snide remarks of my peers, I conducted my interviews sitting at his desk . . . having first arranged the door, half-open, so the inscription MR. BEARD wasn't readily visible. I knew that for the girl I ultimately hired, there would be a day of reckoning, but hoped that when this happened she would be enamored by my wit, personality and $28 a week.

Priscilla had by far the best qualifications . . . big laughing eyes, full sensuous lips, and a figure that curved enticingly in all the right places. She babbled on about her college degrees — one at Stephens and another at North Carolina, in Sociology. Not having attended college, I wasn't too clear just what Sociology involved, but assured her it was exactly the background needed, and gave her the job.

Priscilla wasn't the greatest secretary, but her obvious qualifications caused all the young men in the various related departments to be most cooperative and helpful in getting our work through, no doubt neglecting other worthy souls. Occasionally a feeling of guilt over such unfairness would well up in me, but I always managed to keep it under control.

As a recent widower I will admit to occasional romantic rumblings. But she was fourteen years younger than I. She lived in Tudor City with her younger sister, a gorgeous creature who became a most successful actress. Believe me, they were a couple of charmers that didn't need an old retread like me pursuing them, not for a moment. And I had been sufficiently hurt by the vagaries of life, and didn't want to collect any more bruises for a while. So I played in my own backyard. Or tried to.

But we had things like Christmas parties the company sponsored. I escorted Priscilla to one shortly after she joined McGraw-Hill. And this dialogue ensued — s'help me!

"Miss White, what will you have to drink?"

"Hm-m-m . . . what do they have?"

"Oh, martinis . . . Manhattans . . . ."

"I'll have one of each, and see which I like best!"

I realized then the amount of missionary work that was ahead of me.

One time a colleague of mine and I took Priscilla and her sister to lunch on a Sunday afternoon. We were seated in the outdoor patio of a fine restaurant on Park Avenue, and spring was in the air . . . the season when hopes and dreams sometimes reach reality.

My friend, who is about my age, looked at the two girls, glowing with youthful charm, and said, "Lloyd, what say we send the girls to camp this year." Funny.

I had one other date with Priscilla — a genuine dinner-date, with dancing, at the Coque Rouge, my favorite place, and damn the expense. When I appeared at her apartment, she introduced me to a drama instructor from Yale, who was supposed to have a date with her sister . . . who hadn't appeared.

Priscilla had invited him to join "our group."

He added a great deal to the evening, she later told me, because he was an excellent dancer. We also learned a lot because he was most loquacious and enhanced the evening all around. He also enhanced my check. *C'est la guerre.* And a big *coup de grâce* to our incipient romance. She drifted out of my life and I didn't see her for over two years . . . when we were immediately married.

16

Old people, or, pardon me, "senior citizens," at times looked especially sad to me, when I encountered them in strange corners of the world, clutching their cameras and tote bags. For such trips cost a great deal of money, and it is frequently late in life when couples, with children grown and retirement at hand, are able to finally venture forth with their pre-paid tickets, medications and high hopes. I've seen many such, numb with exhaustion, standing mutely as a guide points out the beauties of a Gothic cathedral, which looks very much like three others they have already seen. Their feet must hurt and there are no doubt many times when they yearn for the comfort of that little house in Peoria, Keokuk or wherever.

The fault is frequently that people desire to cram as many countries and attractions as possible into the relatively few days they can afford for the expedition. For when they return home, there will always be some friend or neighbor who will expostulate, "What — you were in *Italy* and you didn't go to *Florence*? Why it's only the most beautiful city in the *world*!"

Florence *is* beautiful, I am told. I have never been there, having visited only Milan, Rome, and Venice. (Yes, I *know* Capri is a *must*!) I have also never been to Lisbon, Ankara, and Angkor Wat. You must tell me about them. And I'd love to see the slides Clyde took.

I was entering the lobby of the Hilton in Istanbul one time and noted an excited group clustered around an elderly lady, prostrate, on a couch. She was one of a large tour group and had collapsed in exhaustion. In fact, she was dead.

* * *

In planning a world trip with Priscilla not so long ago, I had included

129

several "respites." Oh, those glorious days on the island of Rhodes, in a lovely cottage by the Mediterranean ... as I sat and sipped a highball and watched the white cruise ships glide by. All this while Priscilla was astride a small mule, climbing up to view some ancient site. But then, as I have perhaps noted, she is fourteen years younger than I.

Priscilla always enjoyed such sightseeing sidetrips. She is naturally curious, loquacious, and interested in the finer things of life ... things she calls *objets d'art* but which always turn out to be old cracked vases, faded glass fragments and such. She has several university degrees and I never got beyond a Brooklyn high school, so it is a rare opportunity for me to "expand my horizons." I believe that's the way she puts it.

Before, and during a trip, Priscilla does considerable investigation concerning historical happenings. Thus when she looks at something, she frequently knows more of the nuances than the tourist guide, and sometimes generously supplements his discourse, correcting errors in dates when heads were lopped off or ancient aqueducts built.

My normal tendency is to give such memorabilia a sweeping glance, which absorbs all I really care to know about the subject at hand. Our marital bliss is thus occasionally threatened, particularly as we approach the cocktail hour and I find myself tottering about on some ancient rubble, far from the basic needs of contemporary civilization.

Sometimes she vocally wonders why we ever got married. She points to her lack of companionship while visiting old castles or attending lectures on early Mayan culture. My experience has taught me that the only sure gambit in such discussions is *complete agreement*. I am abjectly aware and deeply sensitive to her embarrassment when she is with other wives, whose husbands are briskly snapping pictures or taking voluminous notes as the guide points out primitive inscriptions that are no longer visible on walls that have long since crumbled.

Of course, we have three sons that secure our marriage. But actually there is one other tie. It brought us together in the first place, and perhaps helps to continue that juxtaposition.

We both like Gilbert and Sullivan, and can burst into song at any moment ... she, one of the twenty lovesick maidens, I a pirate king. I also sing a rather sensitive Ralph Rackstraw ... "Oh pity, pity me ..." (Priscilla, of course, is the captain's daughter). And my Koko to her Yum Yum is not wholly devoid of merit.

But I guess the song that brings us closest is from an old operetta, and concerns the reason why I — love — you. We sing it in tender harmony:

> When I ask the reason
> Words are all too few
> For I know I love you, dear
> Because you're you.

What better reason? Let psychologists, sociologists and such sift the motivations and write searching analyses. But not for me!

It may seem like drastically changing the subject when I mention conventions at this point, but it really isn't. For it was at a convention in Chicago that Priscilla and I again met, after two years.

She had joined the Red Cross and had been sent to England. While there, she had encountered a charming and handsome English officer, John Passmore. Their mutual interest, I suspect, was something more than casual.

But the war was over, and the Red Cross, unromantic clods, insisted she return to Davenport, Iowa, from whence she came . . . while John retired to Tunbridge Wells, to join his father's law firm.

I had inadvertently discovered that Davenport is not far from Chicago, where I had to attend the Music Industry Convention. The faint flame that had always smouldered began to send up smoke signals. I wrote her a note on the letterhead of my very own advertising agency, listing Lloyd W. Dunn, President . . . and suggested she visit Chicago and we run through a few rondos from "Rudigore."

Her train pulled into the Chicago station. I waited, harboring mixed emotions, for two years can make many changes in people.

There she was, still lovely and vivacious. And there was I, no longer the insecure widower, but a man of achievement and purpose!

I proposed marriage in the cab on the way to her hotel. Through two days of 90° midsummer humidity, I pressed my soggy suit, ignoring the convention in which I had been invited to participate, with all expenses paid by Capitol Records, my major client.

A very few weeks later, I found myself playing the leading role in a high-budget production. I stood there in my frock coat and ascot, clutching a top hat that I dared not wear for it was too small . . . and surrounded by handsome young men and lovely ladies, in a crowded church. I, the middle-aged bridegroom, marrying the local belle to a chorus of, "But who *is* he?" I wasn't anybody, especially, but I was very happy.

We don't sing much Gilbert and Sullivan anymore. But I still whisper words of endearment, when I can detach her ear from the telephone. And we get along very well . . . perhaps just "because you're you."

* * *

Another place I had scheduled as a "rest stop" on our world tour was in Spain. We arrived in Barcelona from Amsterdam for an overnight stay, then on to Marbella in Costa del Sol. But first I wanted to visit Monserrat, a monastery high in the hills, noted for its famed "Black Virgin."

For some reason the term "Black Virgin" had always fascinated me. I was under the impression that this was perhaps an attempt at early integration. Or maybe the work had been done by a wandering Moor, who had been coaxed by the Inquisition into changing his faith.

No such thing. The simple fact is that the smoke from endless candles have encrusted the Virgin with layers of black soot. Perhaps the vigorous application of any of the detergents you see featured on television would restore white supremacy. But, no doubt, it would also eliminate a lucrative tourist attraction.

Southern Spain was relaxing and quiet at our hotel on the sea. We saw little night life, perhaps, as Priscilla pointed out, because we didn't get out of the hotel at night. My policy has always been, when traveling with my wife, to relax and enjoy each other's company, away from the pressures of home, the kiddies and the Ecology Club. When I lack the priceless commodity of her company, traveling on business, I catch up on night clubbing with my colleagues.

It has always seemed strange to me that most women lack the capacity to recognize the merits of such an attitude. Priscilla's favorite routine is "We'll never again be here." Sometimes it is varied . . . "I had my hair done, got all dressed up, and *here we sit*."

I point out that one night club is much like another ("With Flamenco dancers?" she says). Prices are excessive, and many clubs are not appropriate places to bring one's wife — the girls there resent it. I have never won any such arguments, and am well aware that a fresh approach is indicated.

Perhaps because I have been in the entertainment business for many years, I find night clubs a drag. To confirm this conviction, I have visited many such establishments throughout the world, some many times, to assure a fair evaluation.

A dramatic example was one cold winter's night in Vienna. For almost a week I had been in Zurich with a business associate, Bud Fraser. We had been participating in a cloak-and-dagger negotiation involving three countries, a large group of executives and many problems. The affair had just been concluded, to our satisfaction, and we needed a little relaxation. As Bud put it, "Where's the action?"

At the risk of alienating some of my Swiss friends, may I say that "the action" is not in Zurich. Scenery, yes — a gorgeous lake, surrounded by snowcapped mountains, studded with quaint chateaus. Right out of the opening scene of an operetta, just before the peasants come leaping on stage.

But we had been in a hotel room for five days. Glued to telephones. Every night all the glorious scenery disappeared into darkness, and the peasants, solid citizens all, locked up their daughters, leaving only a few wandering trolls on the streets.

So we wound up in Vienna, land of music and song. But I learned, to my chagrin, that the famed opera house was closed and music could be

heard only at night clubs. Bud regarded this as a most fortunate hap-
penstance, but he lacks my appreciation of some of the finer manifesta-
tions of cultural endeavor.

Anyhow, we had a few good drinks, a superb dinner, and found
ourselves wandering around an unfamiliar part of town. Actually the
whole city was unfamiliar to us, but this area was especially so, perhaps
because the snow was falling, the wind was picking up, and it began to
get *cold*.

Then looming up in the darkness was a pink neon sign, with a soft
halo around it, glowing through the falling snow. The sign marked the
location of a sort of inn, called "Eve."

"Let's go in for a few minutes and warm up," Bud said. I agreed,
realizing that this was no place for either of us to come down with
chills and fever, with so much work ahead Monday, in Munich.

My first impression of "Eve" was not unfavorable. There was the
traditional bar up front, but toward the rear was another bar tended by
two girl-bartenders dressed, for some inexplicable reason, as French
maids with short black skirts, black stockings and little white lace caps.

To avoid the draft from the door, we moved to the back, where we
were warmly greeted. Actually we were the only customers back there,
so we each had the undivided attention of our own French maid. The
service was excellent. When we came within hailing distance of the
bottom of our glasses, they were whisked away and immediately re-
filled.

An orchestra appeared from the shadows and played, appropriately,
a Viennese waltz. I might mention at this point that the Viennese waltz
is one of the things I do rather well. So I found myself whirling about
with my maid, as she expressed gratification at my talent and agility.

When we returned to the bar, I bought her a drink as a gesture of
appreciation. It was some sort of fruity looking juice that girls in night
clubs the world over seem to prefer.

I felt Bud's elbow in my side. He was hissing something about getting
tired. I smiled sympathetically and turned back to my maid, who, at
this point, had grabbed my arm in clutching affection. When I was
finally able to disengage myself, Bud had gone.

It was not too long after that when I noticed that any other revelers
must have left with Bud. There were three men sitting with their hats
on in the corner, the band was putting away their instruments, and my
maid was again clutching my arm.

With difficulty, I bared my wristwatch. It was 4:00 A.M. Fun is fun,
but my obligation to Capitol rose to the fore and I asked for a check.
The bill was in the area of fifty dollars, a bit on the high side for a few
drinks, I thought, but one must pay the piper. I extracted my billfold,
placed the payment on the tray, and was about to reward the girl with

some small token of my appreciation, when she again clutched my arm. It was my wallet arm, making it impossible to replace the money in my pocket. She had amazing strength for such a little girl.

"And a hundred dollars for me," she said.

My first inclination was to feel that she was confused with currency and exchange involvements. I assumed a paternal smile and said, "You mean in Austrian money."

No. It seemed I was an American and should pay in American money. It was a matter of principle.

"Why should I pay you a hundred dollars?" I asked. "What for?"

"Conversation," she said.

I am by nature a generous man. And I had adequate funds with me. But I had a distinct feeling I was being imposed upon.

So I expressed my feelings to her. Perhaps I did it with a bit too much emphasis, for I recall stating that her services would not be worth a hundred dollars, even if pursued to a relationship considerably more intimate than a Viennese waltz.

This angered her. "I will speak to them," she said, gesturing toward the three men in the corner.

I might mention that these men all wore felt hats with large brims . . . suggesting that they had just stepped from the cast of an old George Raft movie. She leaned over and spoke to them. The three hat brims tilted up. Eyes fixed me, momentarily. Then the three brims dropped. She came back. Her comment could not be classified as a surprise. "They say you should pay me a hundred dollars," she said.

When I inquired the interest of the three men in our personal problem, she told me that one was the owner. The second, more muscular, his aide. And the third . . . he was her husband.

An emotion welled up in me, similar, no doubt, to the way Custer felt when he started counting the Indians. But perhaps I was more of a strategist than the late general. And I had no intention of going down fighting. The very thought of it made me ill.

I slipped off the bar stool and ambled toward the door. Through my peripheral vision I noted that all felt hats were rampant. She helped me on with my overcoat, retaining a firm hold on one sleeve.

As I reached for the door, I took her hand and squeezed it around a ten dollar bill, previously extracted for this ploy. Holding her hand, so she could not inspect my largess, I said brightly, "You've been a good kid. It's been fun." Then I bolted through the door for my escape. Unfortunately it was midwinter and there was an outer vestibule, so I actually bolted through two doors.

Outside a blizzard was raging, and to this day I am grateful for it. Because I galloped off into the clouds of snow, twisting and turning my way through many small, narrow streets. Then, I gasped for breath, hesitated, listening for pursuit . . . half expecting to hear the "Third Man Theme" in the background.

Silence greeted me — blessed silence. Then I realized that snow muffles footsteps, so I kept moving.

As I hurried on, I assessed my situation. It was well after 4:00 A.M. Not a soul was in sight. I was in a strange city, and worse, didn't know where I was or how to get back to the hotel.

I wandered through the maze of streets, hoping that I would not suddenly find myself back in front of "Eve's" neon sign. As the snow died off, and the roseate tint of dawn was reflected in the whiteness, I arrived at the hotel. I was dead tired, wet and cold, but somehow triumphant.

17

As we were about to board our Air India flight from Singapore to Calcutta, Keith handed me the largest bottle of Scotch I have ever seen. I didn't know it was retailed in such a mammoth model.

Then I noted Bill Stanford embracing a similar jug of Gordon's gin. It seems that India is a dry country and getting even one small libation for a parched throat involves more supplication and paper work than it's worth. Or almost.

But visitors are allowed to bring in *one* bottle. I suspected that the regulations did not cover my King Kong container, but I was assured that there would be no problem at customs.

Keith Brice, head of EMI's Singapore company, is an Englishman who bears a striking resemblance to David Niven, the actor. I occasionally admit to a night club hostess that he is traveling incognito . . . it seems to bring us special favors. And the "authenticity" of his identity is seemingly made positive by his denials.

Our mentor on this expedition was Bhaskar Menon. He was EMI's top executive in India, and had all the requisites for a full and colorful life . . . good looking, a great personality and wit, youngish, a member of the illustrious Menon family of India, and an Oxford "Blue." Bhaskar was recently happily married to an Indian beauty who can match his charm, quip for quip. But at that time his hobby was airline stewardesses and he had a splendid collection. Included of course, were the more available Air India, BOAC, Pan Am and TWA species. But beyond that, there were myriad colorful specimens, even from far-off feeder lines: truly an example of what diligence and constant application can achieve, if one starts young.

It is said that when in his spacious house in Calcutta, Bhaskar would cock his head as a plane passed high above, and mutter, "Dorothy!" —

or Suri, or Gretchen or . . . well, the list is impressive. Shortly thereafter his phone would ring in charming confirmation.

When we arrived at the crowded airport, I distinguished myself by leaving my bottle of Scotch on the plane. I am not used to transporting liquor in such vulgar quantities and I didn't even think of it until I noticed Bill Stanford clutching his jug like a nursing mother. I mentioned the oversight, and Bhaskar sprang into action. Minutes later a local attendant was chattering through a walkie-talkie to the plane, and shortly thereafter the bottle was placed in my outstretched arms. (Gentlemen of Air India, I salute you!)

The next evening there was a big party at the hotel in our honor. People in the music business came from far and wide to meet us. I had understood that Indians were mostly abstainers, but they munched hors d'oeuvres and toasted our health with growing enthusiasm.

I was really touched by the warmth of their greetings, and my emotions cooled only a few degrees when I learned that Bhaskar was serving *my* Scotch, it being unavailable at the hotel. The guests had drained the bottle to the last drop, like music men the world over.

And all this time, Stanford's gin was locked up in his room. He lacks my basic social graces.

* * *

While in Calcutta I learned that it was the season for some sort of music festival. The populace pretty much deify Saraswathi, the Goddess of Music, and during the celebration thousands of devotees purchase clay statues of "Sara," in varying sizes and degrees of ornamentation — some quite large and handsomely colored. At the end of the week the images are taken down to the Ganges and cast into it. I assume the clay dissolves and is washed away.

As an international music executive, I was apparently extended special honors which, though not quite clear, were impressive. After being driven through a maze of crowded streets, we stopped before a large two-story building. Here I was warmly greeted by a small group, who escorted me to a spacious chamber on the upper floor. The room, which was perhaps a recording studio, contained a huge and handsomely decorated statue of Saraswathi, in sparkling display, illuminated by spotlights overhead.

I was escorted to a position directly in front of the impressive figure, as everyone moved back into the shadows, leaving me in a position for solitary contemplation.

No one had given me my "routine," so I stood in reverent silence, wondering whether I should fall prone in abject adoration, or perhaps a limited genuflection would be adequate. Flashbulbs popping in the background convinced me that an immediate decision was essential, so I settled on dropping my head slightly and closing my eyes, obviously in deep meditation. Then I straightened up, turned and rejoined the group, hoping that I had acquitted myself well.

It was then that I was escorted out on a balcony, overlooking the street below. Much to my surprise, I found a sea of faces, all looking up in glowing anticipation. Apparently I had already been introduced as something special because, as a microphone was pushed in front of me, the crowd quieted.

At this point I hadn't the foggiest idea of who I was supposed to be or what I was expected to say. And there was no time for a briefing. I affected what I hoped was a benign expression I had once seen on the face of Pope John, in a newsreel, as he blessed the multitudes. The crowd waited respectfully for my *pax vobiscum.*

I gave them an abbreviated version of "Music — the International Language of Peace." I've delivered it many times in all sorts of places, including Moscow, and it has always been well received. For it contains nothing that could possibly offend anyone, however bigoted, and the theme is noble and uplifting.

This was no exception. I got a warm reception, and my sensitivities were only slightly bruised when I learned that few among my avid audience understood English. Indians are very courteous people.

* * *

Speeches given before audiences who don't understand English present unique problems. In Japan, for example, where I made many talks, I have learned through embarrassing experience never to deviate from the tried and true clichés used, no doubt, by Admiral Perry, when he opened the country to world trade. For the interpreter is rarely facile with your language and he must relay *thoughts* rather than words. Clichés are comfortable — old friends that can be nicely packaged and delivered to an audience, who should know their intent — they've heard them enough.

In my early visits to Japan, I used to make some awfully clever remarks — comments that had rolled them in the aisles in the States. When the interpreter's face would not brighten at my *bons mots*, I would get uneasy. When he hesitated a moment, then delivered in eight seconds what had taken me three minutes to say, I would watch, waiting for that mass show of teeth and explosive guffaws.

Nothing. Dead silence.

"It loses something in the translation." It always does. Everything.

Yet every businessman, even if only moderately successful, usually finds himself in a situation where he *must* get up on his hind legs before a group of his peers and *say something*. It may be only at the National Pigs' Liver Distributors Convention, where he has just received the

Ramaki Award for Product Development. Here, for the first time, he is looking not at the familiar backs of heads, but at a sea of faces and *eyes*.

His mouth opens and he is startled to hear a strange sound . . . his voice? He tries to avoid his audience by looking at the floor or ceiling. He stuffs both hands in his pockets, eliminating the possibility of all normal gestures.

A few people at the rear of the room shout for him to speak *louder* — they can't understand his mumblings. When he does they have reason to regret it. For while his mouth is moving his brain is obviously not in gear. He looks terrified because he is.

The foregoing paragraph could be labeled "Portrait of Dunn" in the early thirties, the middle of the Depression.

I was fortunate, during this dreadful doldrum, to land two half-time jobs. One was from nine until one, in uptown Manhattan. The other was from one till five, way downtown. The logistics were obviously insuperable. I alternated, leaving the morning job early one day, and arriving at the afternoon job late the next day. Thus I was bawled out alternately, but not fired. As for lunch, I packed a sandwich at home, and ate it sitting in the privacy of a booth in the men's room.

But then came that Golden Moment when a friend, Roger Knight, bless him, got me a job at McGraw-Hill. Just one *full*-time job, and paying sixty dollars a week! And a whole hour for lunch, in comfort and clean air.

In humble gratitude, I worked hard and long. And ultimately, came the moment when I was given some sort of award and had to make a speech of acceptance.

Never will I forget walking into the huge office of the Executive Vice-President. Strangely enough, I could not hear my footsteps. Looking down, to be sure I had my feet with me, I found them buried in the lush carpet.

What followed I wish I could forget . . . mumbling, stumbling, bumbling. Strange how failures remain more vivid in memory than achievements.

A few days later I went to Dale Carnegie and laid down a good portion of my luncheon budget for a course in public speaking. Then, night after night, for many weeks, instructors tried to beat the shyness out of me and teach me to "think on my feet."

I recall a device they used to develop dramatic emphasis and violent gestures. At every session, each student had to step on the stage and address the audience, using this one paragraph, which I remember to this day . . .

"I know men in the ranks who will *remain* in the ranks. Why? *I'll* tell you why! Simply because they lack the capacity to *GET THINGS DONE!!!*"

I got pretty good at it, but unfortunately was never able to work the phrase into a business discussion. But I did do a good deal of public speaking, and as I gained confidence, really began to enjoy it.

Priscilla also likes to make speeches. She lacks some of my nuances, perhaps, but compensates by being better looking. Today she is a militant ecologist. One of her well-received talks is "Give Our Coastline Back to the People," which depresses me somewhat because I own a lot right on the water in San Diego and was kind of looking forward to having my sailboat moved up to the front patio.

I can honestly say her best talk was in Tokyo, not long ago. We were on a round-the-world trip together, and visited our Japanese associates in Japan. Toshiba's Board of Directors held a dinner in our honor. Traditionally, Japanese executives do not include their wives at such affairs, and it was a special tribute to Priscilla that she was included — the only woman present.

The dinner was long and elaborate, as we went from room to room for each succulent course. We wound up for liqueurs in a large room, where we were presented with gifts. I then made a speech, thanking everyone and expressing my high regard for them . . . a genuinely sincere statement, for Mr. Suga and his staff are honorable and capable businessmen, and we have prospered together.

Priscilla tugged at my sleeve and announced that *she* wanted to speak. Before I had a chance to whisper "Cool it, baby!" she was on her feet and babbling away.

Her theme concerned my many trips to the Orient. She quoted my remarks to her concerning the beauty and charm of Japanese women. I had been under the impression that I had been cautious in making such observations at home. Perhaps I talk in my sleep. In any event it was all too true. I have fallen in love with many Japanese girls whose names I forget because they consist of strange tangles of letters, but whose beauty will warm my memory through my declining years.

Priscilla was developing her theme. I was growing increasingly uneasy. But then she arrived at the payoff.

It seems she had wondered about Japanese *men*. And now that she had been granted the opportunity to be with so many of them on such an occasion, she could forever speak with ringing authority. For they, too, were handsome, charming . . . and on she went.

She finished to loud applause and shouts of approval. We had another drink all around and the party wound up with all these dignified executives joining in a circle, arms on shoulders, and bursting into a spirited chant that sounded like the Fight Song of Tokyo Tech, but I suspect was a special tribute to their honored guests. It was a memorable evening, one we will never forget.

* * *

Priscilla has an opening story that she sometimes uses — not quite as raunchy as some of mine. It concerns a Ph.D. in a small college town. He purchases a power lawn mower, through mail order, and is trying to assemble it on his front lawn. After several futile efforts, concerning things like inserting Bolt R into Hole E (there *is* no hole E!), the professor is ready to cut his wrists with the mower blades. Then Henry, the local handyman, passes and looks over the gate. Moments later, Henry has the machine together and running smoothly.

"Henry," says the professor, "how can you accomplish such wonders with little or no formal education?"

Henry quickly answers, "When you can't *read* and you can't *write*, you gotta *think*!"

* * *

My round-the-world trip with Priscilla included the Kashmir region of India, one of the loveliest areas in the world. Ah, that lovely lake . . . you glide through it propelled by an invisible gondolier-like chap, as you recline on soft cushions — sensuous, voluptuous, sybaritic — comfortable! I was slipping into a Rajahish mood, with Priscilla selected from my assorted wives for the afternoon dalliance . . .

Then a boat slithered up, loaded to the gunwales with assorted merchandise. With a princely gesture I was going to have the vendor boiled in oil — slowly. But the spell was broken. Priscilla, who like most women has a passion for shopping — anywhere, anytime, anything — bought fur-lined chamois gloves, never worn in California, but for only two dollars! (And they were labeled, "Made in Israel"!) Apparently the floating emporium was going to cling to us until I also made a purchase so I asked him for a cough remedy, which I had neglected to include in our medical kit. Much to my surprise, he reached deep among the assorted gimcracks and came up with as fine a bottle of Vicks Cough Medicine as you could buy at your neighborhood drugstore. I was tempted to ask him for a carburetor for an old Chevy my son was attempting to fix, but I knew he would have it, and transportation would be a problem.

When we got back to the hotel, Priscilla immediately left for a tour of some nearby gardens. I was exhausted from my expedition on the lake, and decided to crawl under the covers for a nap, to restore my strength for the cocktail hour.

Our room boy, anticipating my every need, had turned down the covers and drawn the drapes. I slipped off my garments and was about to wiggle into bed when I hesitated.

I know this is going to sound silly to you, but years ago I read a story — perhaps by Kipling — that concerned an interesting propensity of cobras. On occasion, they have been known to slither under the covers for the same reason people do — to get warm and comfortable. While there is no malice aforethought involved, the fact remains that when two bare feet are suddenly thrust into the coils of the cobra, he resents it. No doubt a certain amount of conflict ensues which is not conducive to relaxation and rest.

I remember an Englishman telling me that when he was with the army in India, they always turned their boots bottoms up before putting them on . . . to eject "visitors." (Maybe that's where the expression "Die with your boots on" comes from.)

I don't know why snakes fascinate and terrify me at the same time but they do. Priscilla eyes them casually, and near Agra posed with a huge python draped around her like a mink stole, while I snapped her picture. My photo of this scene has received critical comment because it is not a closeup. It was close enough for me.

So perhaps you will understand my momentary fear, as I looked at those open covers . . . and hesitated.

But then I said to myself, "Lloyd, old boy, you must learn to control your childish imaginings." And I leaped happily under the covers.

It was then that my bare feet struck something strange. It was soft. And warmish. And it moved when I pushed against it.

To say that I got out of bed at this juncture would not do justice to my agility. I shot out of bed like men are shot from cannons at the circus. And I stood trembling in a most uncontrollable fashion.

When I regained some composure, I rang for the room boy, and told him, in essence, there was a cobra under my covers. He seemed quite calm about the whole thing. Perhaps the place was crawling with the creatures and the incident routine. With quiet courage, he flipped down the covers.

There was my cobra. A plump red one. A hot water bag, inserted just before my arrival at the room, for my cozy comfort.

I must say at this point that at *no time time in all my life* had anyone put a hot water bottle in my bed. I never even *saw* one before. As a boy, such luxuries were not available to us . . . in later affluence, electric blankets were obtainable.

So when my tired feet encountered a soft, squishy, moving object, my reaction was *not* childish or cowardly, as Priscilla later inferred. It was an uncontrollable reflex!

Our houseboy continued to be courteous, respectful and helpful, but I had a conviction that when he met with the other houseboys, the laughter was loud, and at my expense. If *I* had been a houseboy I would have urged, "Now let's put a *real* cobra in and he'll think it's a hot water bottle!"

18

It seems that wherever you are in the world, the procedure of registering at a hotel is pretty much the same. I have grown inured to it. But I have seen less experienced travelers reduced to tearful entreaties that are most touching.

The Desk Clerk, if I may so designate such a distinguished gentleman, looks away, with a faint shudder, as you lurch up to the counter, disheveled and tired from your long journey. Despite his obvious lack of interest in the whole sordid business, travelers speak up in hopefully questioning tones. Not me.

"You *have* a reservation for Lloyd Dunn."

I say this not as a question, but as a statement of *unassailable fact*.

He *always* turns away, his very posture suggests a lack of faith in my basic integrity. He *always* flips through a number of cellophane-clad cards, clinging to a wall file of some sort, like bats in a cave. He starts making little clucking noises of reproof. Of course he doesn't find you. He never expected to.

As the next required gambit, he always disappears into a back room. There is a general feeling among travelers that his mission is to seek out your name which has either been misplaced or is on an executive desk, marked for special consideration. My experience has taught me that what he probably does in these outer recesses is to engage in chitchat with the girl in the miniskirt who handles billing. Lacking that, he takes advantage of this respite to trim his fingernails and brush back a few errant locks of hair. The point to remember is that he entered the room not to help you, but to get away from you.

Ultimately he returns, lifting his arms and then dropping them to his sides in a gesture of futility. If he does speak, he always says, "*Who* made the reservation?"

I suppose the average answer from the average guest is "The Marco Polo Travel Agency in Sabre Tooth, Idaho." This enables him to smile condescendingly and make a paternal suggestion regarding possible accommodations at a small establishment at the other end of the city . . . next to the glue factory.

But at this point I frequently look directly into his beady black eyes and say, "Sir Joseph Lockwood, Chairman of EMI. May I use your phone to call his home?"

This stratagem is often sufficient for him to thrust a registration card at me in sullen surrender. But not always.

Like the time I arrived in London, on a late plane, delayed by storms and headwinds. EMI had a car waiting at the airport and the chauffeur dropped me, shortly after midnight, in a heavy rain, at the elegant Woodbury . . . small but distinguished.

The doorman had disappeared to more comfortable quarters, so I staggered into the lobby, dropped my bags and approached the line of battle. The standard routine followed, different only in that the clerk was conscientious and inspected a wider variety of files. They were all arranged alphabetically and it was plain to see there was no reservation under D for Dunn.

My EMI routine fell on deaf ears.

"We have *no* rooms available at this time, sir," he intoned as he disappeared through a rear door, ending the possibility of further discussion.

I debated for one glorious moment taking off everything down to my shorts and stretching out on the sumptuous couch in the lobby. Then I picked up my bags and splashed off into the night, with the rain falling in huge globs, driven by a cold wind.

After a brief eternity, I encountered a cab. "Where to, sir?" he said cheerfully. Bless the London taxis for their spacious comfort and the cabbies for their courtesy. I considered for a moment retaining the cab for the night, then decided to operate on the theory that there was always room at the top.

"The Dorchester," I said.

You may know that the Dorchester is surely London's finest in traditional English hotels. In every way it always seems to justify the strain it puts on one's budget, and it is always booked solid months ahead.

The doorman was still on duty at 2:00 A.M., tall and handsome in his top hat, and encouraging in his warm reception. He escorted me to the desk like visiting nobility. I decided to play it straight and throw myself at the desk clerk's mercy, so I told him the whole story including the Woodbury's shabby treatment.

He had *one* room. At such times, this is not infrequently a hotel maneuver during which you are compelled to accept the Royal Suite at a royal price. But in this case it was quite the opposite. The "only room" was a remote cubicle without a private bath, used by the butlers or maids traveling with an entourage. Obviously aware of my status, he was most apologetic.

I accepted, with gratitude. And how cozy the room looked on that wet, cold night . . . neat and clean, with a thick comforter on the bed and steam or water pipes running decoratively across the ceiling. Loverly! I slept a blessed sleep and happily paid my eight dollars for the room the next day, following my seven dollar breakfast.

EMI exploded when they heard my sad story. They sent a representative to the Woodbury, carrying a figurative mace and ready to swing it. I wanted to go along, for on such occasions I enjoy the sight of blood, but business engagements prevented it.

After considerable conversation in cloistered offices, perhaps with Mr. Woodbury himself, the mystery was solved. Of course, they had my reservation! There it was, properly recorded under W, for Lloyd Wyatt-Dunn!

Yes, that *is* my middle name. I didn't know EMI was aware of it, for I haven't used it since my mother insisted it appear on my high school diploma. In England names are sometimes hyphenated, and so this touch of distinction was added by the Woodbury to my reservation. It didn't occur to the mutton-headed room clerk to look at the reservations of *all* guests who had not yet arrived at that late hour, after midnight. The whole exercise would have been too exhausting.

A similar incident occurred, of all things, on my honeymoon. We were married in great splendor in Davenport, Iowa, where Priscilla's father was a prominent doctor, and she and her sister, Patricia, the local belles. I had difficulty living up to the leading role in this high-budget production, and was relieved when we drove off to the airport to the cheers of innumerable friends and relatives.

Our plan was to fly to the Edgewater Beach Hotel in Chicago, where we had reserved a suite for the night, departing the next day for Lake Tahoe, California, for our honeymoon.

But when we arrived at the airport we were greeted by the amazing announcement that the plane, which usually hopped to Chicago in less than an hour, would be *three hours* late!

Nothing to do but sneak back to her house and remain in hiding until plane time — an awkward anticlimax.

So we finally arrived at the Edgewater Beach about 2:00 A.M. — where I faced the same miserable routine — *no reservation*.

I told the clerk that we had just been married, but he regarded my statement with suspicion, and in any event not his problem, insensitive, unromantic lout that he was.

I rose to new heights of eloquence. I stormed. I shouted. I finally went behind the desk, over his loud protests, and reviewed the list myself.

We were there, all right. The reservation was under the name of Mrs. Paul A. White, Priscilla's mother, who had phoned it in from Davenport. I've always accused her of planning to go along on the honeymoon. She and Priscilla are very close.

*　*　*

It all reminds me of my first honeymoon, if Priscilla will forgive this juxtaposition. In the pit of the Depression, stone broke, I had married a bright-eyed charmer from Syracuse, Doris Wilcox, who was studying to be a nurse at Fifth Avenue Hospital in New York. Our romance was conducted through the shadowy walks and secluded benches of Central Park, where now I am told it is dangerous to venture after dark. How sad for today's young lovers, trapped in the cement and brick of a big city.

Doris, sweet soul, came up with the money for a honeymoon to Bermuda, because she said that if we didn't go right then, we never would. Death proved her to be so right.

We sailed on the beautiful "Monarch of Bermuda" — four days of luxury, round trip for only sixty dollars each. And that included gourmet meals!

To counterbalance this extravagance, we had reservations at a modest hotel for four dollars a day. But it appeared, when we got acquainted with a fellow passenger, that our hotel was hardly suitable for honeymooners, being situated in the business section of Hamilton, and generally occupied by traveling sales people.

The Inveraray Hotel was *the* place, we were told ... lovely and white, right on the water, dancing every night ... yummy! We took a deep breath and switched to this hotel, feeling well over our heads socially and financially, for we agreed not to ask the rate, lest it cloud our two-day stay.

Ah, those dear dead days. We were received graciously, escorted to a charming room, with high ceilings and French windows overlooking the bay. The swimming was sensational, the food fabulous, the dancing delightful, our love boundless. All our dreams came true for a total of six dollars a day! It was well worth the difference, we agreed.

I wonder if two such young people, wide-eyed with wonderment, entered that lobby today, would they be subject to the "no reservation" routine and the casual indifference. I like to think it is still the same, and at times have been tempted to return ... knowing full well that I must not, for nothing stays the same as the years pass ... except memories.

*　*　*

One night I arrived in Honolulu, from Tokyo, after a long rough flight. I was with Bill Stanford, a top executive with EMI, and as fine a gentleman as I have ever known. It was a weekend and we had decided to relax for two days at the magnificent Kahala Hilton, in the shadow of Diamond Head, far from Waikiki Beach, with its surging sea of muumuus and Aloha shirts. I had made the reservations from Hong Kong.

We debarked in a real tropical downpour and managed to absorb a good share of it before tumbling into a cab with our baggage for the long — ten dollars' worth — ride to Kahala.

We entered the elegant lobby, feeling a bit bedraggled and anticipating "a warm bath and a cold martini."

Folks at the Kahala really dress for dinner and are a worthy compliment to the gorgeous accouterments of the lobby. An exquisitely groomed gentleman greeted us at the desk. And here we encountered a new variation on the no-reservations theme.

They did have the reservations, so the damp confirmation clutched in my hand was unnecessary. The rooms, however, were *unavailable*. A shadow of distress passed over the man's visage, and he turned up his palms to heaven in a gesture of abject futility. I must say it was a far superior performance to others I have witnessed. But this was a superior hotel.

But Stanford and Dunn were old hands at the game, not to be turned aside lightly. In loud, vulgar tones we loosed a few well-selected invectives, which threatened to upset some of the sensitive guests in the lobby. And at that point he interrupted to assure us that our welfare had been a matter of prime consideration to the establishment. They had *protected* us!

For the uninitiated, I must explain that when a fancy room clerk has "protected" you, it usually means he has booked you into some flea-trap bordering the industrial area, to make room for a VIP who strolled in unannounced, tossing around first names and bringing memories of previous lavish rewards to those who served him well.

After a twenty-minute wait for a cab, and another ten-dollar cab ride, we arrived at a motel, cheek-and-jowl against the airport. It was jammed with guests, children, baggage and a few pets — all beseeching the solace of a room. It seems that several huge organizations like the Moose, Elks, and perhaps Gnus, had descended upon this Pearl of the Pacific in one sweating swoop, and rooms had been gobbled up.

But our rooms *were* available! We callously elbowed aside old ladies and tripped over sleeping children, finally closing the door on suffering humanity and gloating in the luxury of motel furnishings, with the faint sound of planes landing, departing, and circling overhead.

I have been back to the Kahala several times since, because my past resentment has been more than offset by the charm and luxury of the place. It's one of my less admirable traits — placing my hedonistic inclinations above honor and principle.

* * *

Mexico City and its environs have many impressive hotels, and once one gets used to their charming frailties, a pleasant time can be had.

I recall one fine establishment where I had a suite. It was a strange layout, because the living room and bedroom were connected by a long hall with the general dimensions of a bowling alley. But the service was excellent.

One night, when I went to bed I discovered that a chilling blast from the air conditioning struck me directly in the face, making it necessary to withdraw under the covers where breathing was difficult. I phoned downstairs and a few moments later there was a soft tap-tap at my door. No grimy plumber appeared, but instead a well-groomed gentleman in full uniform, emblazoned with the hotel insignia, carrying a neat kit of tools.

He extracted a screwdriver and removed the top of the air conditioning unit, which was right next to the bed. Then he disappeared in the bathroom, of all places. When he returned he was clutching a large and snowy bath towel, which he wedged into the air conditioning unit before replacing the lid.

Then he turned to me with a smile and bowed slightly. *"Muchas gracias,"* I said. *"Por nada,"* he replied, with a self-deprecating gesture and departed.

No doubt the towel remained for a considerable period, until a hot spell, when a guest complained of no air conditioning, at which point the towel was removed.

Speaking of air conditioning, Priscilla and I once visited Acapulco in late June. In season it's a fun place, but out of season it's hot, sticky, and tropical, as we found out. We were booked into the Club de Pesca, a hotel that looked sensational in a long shot, but when you got close, all those modern architectural features were peeling paint, brown with rust and in a state of mouldy decay that suggested the jungle would ultimately take over, like at Angkor Wat.

We were courteously escorted to a room. But it was blistering. The air conditioning unit, projecting from a window, had no doubt rusted away.

I took the elevator to the lobby, and before I had reached any great emotional heights, was given a key to another room. *Muchas gracias.*

I returned and we moved our baggage to the other room. It was a similar room in every respect except the window air conditioning unit not only wasn't working but was sagging at an angle suggesting imminent departure.

I returned to the field of battle, where I was greeted with that familiar gesture of utter despair, so often encountered in Latin America. The clerk told me to take *any* available room in the hotel, of which there were many. In that huge hotel there was not one room in which the air conditioning worked! We later found that only in the bar was the air cool and refreshing, but they wouldn't let us sleep there.

We went swimming in the pool to cool off. It was like one of those old movie comedies, where they reverse the film suddenly. I jumped into the pool and popped out. It was *hot*. The water in the bay was a bit cooler but it had the consistency of luke-warm chicken soup — cream of chicken.

I went upstairs for a shower. Ours didn't work. With a towel around my middle, I strolled from room to room until I found one that did.

In fairness to Acapulco, I must state that when the season is right, it's delightful. And many new hotels have been built, all, no doubt, completely functional.

* * *

The Maria Isabella Hotel is considered the best in Mexico City. It has a lovely setting, spacious halls, and nicely furnished rooms. My only complaint is with the management. I hate them.

I was on a business trip and I took my young son, Steve, along. He had never been to a foreign country and it was all very exciting. The city was jammed but we had reservations at the Maria Isabella, and it took only a few minor maneuvers to obtain our room ... which was reserved from Monday through Friday night, leaving Saturday. All duly documented at the desk.

But on Friday night about seven, the phone rang in our room. It was the desk clerk downstairs. The dialogue went like this:

"Mr. Dunn? This is the desk. What are you doing in your room?"

He had interrupted a rather intimate activity — they feature phones in the bathroom. So I said coyly, "Why?"

"You should be *out*!" he said. "We need your room!"

"But I have a reservation through Friday night," I said, keeping my voice under admirable control.

"I know about your reservation," he said, with a tone suggesting I was using the room as a headquarters for smuggling narcotics. "But we want your room. Right now!"

"You can't have it," I said, zipping up my trousers.

His reply I can still quote verbatim, because never in my years of travel, in good hotels and bad, have I heard such a remark to a guest.

"Then we'll come up and *throw* you out!" he said, and slammed down the phone.

I quickly advised Steve to gird for battle. Steve had inherited from his father a natural aversion to violence, particularly when one is doomed for defeat. But together we bravely stood, ready to defend the bastion until our yellow streaks ran red.

Then the executive in me rose to the fore. I quickly phoned Victor Rivero, our Mexican business partner, and a man of considerable influence. He expressed no surprise . . . perhaps it was routine. But he said, "Don't worry, I'll handle it."

We did worry, until the telephone rang again. It was my friend, the desk clerk, and his voice bordered on the unctuous.

"Mr. Dunn? You may remain in your room. Enjoy your stay with us."

I could not help feeling sorry for the people who were going to be thrown out in our stead.

* * *

A while back I had to go to Kingston, Jamaica, to work out a problem concerning Capitol's distribution. I was to meet a colleague from England there who had booked into the Sheraton, or some similar large chain hotel. But my travel agent assured me it would be much more enjoyable to stay at a more colorful establishment, the Flaming O. I must admit, it sounded more romantic than the other. He showed me a multicolored folder and I was impressed; beautiful flowers, lovely girls in bikinis lolling around the pool . . . an obvious tropical paradise. I not only booked two rooms for myself and my associate, Dick Rising, but I cabled the Englishman to change his reservation.

We arrived in Jamaica after dark and in due course taxied up to our hotel. It was a rambling two-story structure, a bit shadowy at night. I must admit it had sort of a Somerset Maughamish charm, with an aura of underlying tragedy.

I followed the boy with my bags up the outside stairway to my room. It was obvious that the air conditioning was not working. In fact, I don't believe they had any, for the windows were open. There were screens, but much of the mesh needed attention.

In the center of the ceiling was the white lighting fixture. I fell on the bed, exhausted from the trip, with the light glaring in my eyes.

Then I noticed the ceiling. Starkly illuminated, it appeared to have a great quantity of little shapes on it. They were moving.

Tired as I was, I did not stir, but watched. Most of the bugs were unfamiliar to me. There appeared to be a certain amount of conflict going on . . . perhaps "territorial imperative" at work. An occasional loser dropped on the bed — or me.

There was a knock on the door. It was Dick. "Have you any objection to my grabbing a cab and looking for another place to stay?" he said.

"Count me in," said I, "they're on my ceiling, too."

He returned an hour later and we moved to a sort of motel. It didn't have a romantic name, but it was new and clean, and the air conditioning worked.

The Englishman? He stated that my cable had not arrived, so he had checked into the beautiful, lush Sheraton, where he always stayed. We enjoyed visiting him.

* * *

Fiji always sounded exciting to me, and I welcomed an opportunity for a brief visit. I was headed for Australia, from Honolulu. The flight left at 1:00 A.M. and about six hours later landed in Nandi, Fiji, for refueling. I decided to spend a day and night there, and continue on to Sydney in the morning via Air India.

I had been booked into what had been described as "a hotel on the beach." It had a lot of rambling low structures; the beach was perhaps visible, but I had no binoculars.

I wandered around town most of the day, then slept for a few hours till I was awakened by the pulsation of throbbing drums. Ever curious, I put on a clean shirt and stepped out. The music came from the bar, and I walked over to investigate, as any music lover would.

I must say the place was jumping. I selected a table next to the wall, ordered a Singapore Sling, and leaned back to watch the action. It was really relaxing.

I remember devoting a good portion of my attention to a tall, lovely girl who was dancing with enthusiasm. Her deep tan contrasted with her white dress, and the brief accordian-pleated miniskirt swirled most provocatively as she gyrated in what might be termed a down-under jitterbug.

I was on my second sling when I noticed strange markings on the ceiling. Silly as it sounds, they looked like footprints. I questioned the waiter.

"They *are* footprints," he confirmed. "Ladies' footprints. It's the custom here every time an airline stewardess comes through for the first time, the lads up-end her and stamp her footprints on the ceiling."

It seemed like a jolly custom. I sat there for a long time, but unfortunately all the ladies were habitues. No up-ending.

And the next morning, when I boarded Air India, I was welcomed by a serene young Indian lady in a colorful sari. She bowed to me in stately dignity, her palms together, in her country's traditional greeting.

"Don't give me that routine," I said. "I saw you last night leaping about in a miniskirt!"

Her composure remained unruffled. "And I saw you, too, sir," she said. I told her my view was more intriguing.

* * *

A unique part of the charm of many European hotels is their firm principles about heating and air conditioning. These comforts are applied not based on temperature, but on the calendar. Thus, when it is bitterly cold in April, there will be no — but *no* — heat. And air conditioning will be operating in June during icy rainstorms. Your personal metabolism must defer to the rules.

Consider the Connaught Hotel, regarded by many to be the most exclusive in London. It is so severely traditional that when I first stayed there the ancient elevator — pardon me, *lift* — was activated by a pull on the wire rope, running through the cage . . . like our freight elevators used to function. I have been in the Connaught in icy midwinter when the chambermaid insisted on leaving the windows open all day while I was at work. "It freshens the air, sir," she used to say, overruling my protests.

I used to go to bed early, to keep warm under the huge "comforter" . . . a quilt-like affair that always slid off my bed during the night, leaving me shivering in my sleep. Later I coaxed the housekeeper to bring me something she called a "fire," which proved to be an electric heater with two small tubular elements, which glowed cheerfully but would be effective only if taken under the covers.

But I did see Cary Grant with Ingrid Bergman in the lobby. Also, the cuisine was superb.

And the doorman. Now *there* was a dramatic personage, both in appearance and personality! One sleepy Sunday afternoon I asked him if there were any movie theaters open on Sunday. He named one, adding the editorial comment, "And if I had *my* way, they'd close that!" I slunk off, feeling I was not living up to the Connaught's high standards.

19

May I make one thing absolutely clear at this juncture. I do not like cherries in my Manhattan cocktails.

Repeat: I *do not*. *Please*. Out, out, out!

I mention this because I am told that authors are occasionally invited to cocktail parties, and my hosts may find this the only flaw in an otherwise kind, easygoing, warm and lovable disposition. My wife still tells of the time I dropped the wet red orb on an off-white carpet and ground it in with my heel. She always relates the end result without stating the provocation, which makes me appear loutish. So may I tell *my* side?

Early in my drinking career, when a New Yorker, I developed a fondness for Manhattan cocktails. They were more colorful to look at, less lethal, and did not assault my sensitive taste buds like martinis.

But I found that the delicate flavor was boorishly dominated by the plopping in of a maraschino cherry. In pies I welcome cherries as pleasant and acceptable. The dessert, cherries jubilee, flames with a festive warmth and adds a decorative touch. But that same cherry — or perhaps it is the juice in which it is embalmed — changes the personality of a Manhattan and makes it a simpering liqueur, suitable only for ladies, for after-dinner dawdling. I don't like it. Please leave it out.

Now that seems like a modest request, doesn't it? Martini drinkers go through all kinds of expostulations regarding their preferences. I know one who insists on a large fragment of raw cauliflower in his drinks — he seems to like to munch his cocktail. Having encountered a lack of cauliflower at the average party, he brings it with him . . . a gesture I find socially unacceptable.

But my desire is merely to *eliminate* an ingredient. And, amazingly, that's where I get into so much trouble.

Professional bartenders make drinks in great quantities, frequently under pressure. I suspect they flip an olive into a martini, cherries into Manhattans, and so on, in a reflex action, perhaps uncontrollable. I do know that when I stand at a bar and shout, as hand moves, I frequently get a piece of lemon peel or some other oddment in my drink. Perhaps it is a union rule that *something* must go in.

You may well say, "Why doesn't that clown merely remove the fruit and stop being so unpleasant about it?"

It seems a reasonable request and I have done this on many occasions. But the damage is already done, just as the brine from an olive flavors a martini. And at today's prices it would seem I should get what I order.

One Christmas, my fellow workers who dined with me often, gave me a gift. It comprised five hundred bits of paper, about the size of business cards. On each was a full color picture of a cherry with an "X" across it. The type said, "One Manhattan — *no* cherry, please!" I was truly grateful even after they told me it was more their problem than mine.

Amazingly, the use of these cards seemed to affront the proprietory rights of those involved. To waiters, it perhaps suggested that they lacked the capacity to carry the message to Garcia, the bartender . . . an accurate assumption. In any event, while the cards amused some, they angered most. I have had my card returned on the tray accompanying the cocktail, with the cherry, leering triumphantly through the glass.

Perhaps the ultimate encounter in endless skirmishes occurred on our wedding anniversary several years ago. Priscilla decided we should have a quiet dinner together in a very elegant restaurant . . . "the kind we used to have when we were first married." I selected a very special place in Beverly Hills. It seemed a good choice, for we were greeted by the maitre d', resplendent in tails and starched white, who escorted us to a choice table gleaming in soft candlelight with fine napery, crystal and other elegant accouterments.

"Cocktails before dinner?" he inquired.

I went through my routine, which I had reduced to a few easily understood phrases, throwing in some extra words of apology for being such a bother. The maitre d' held up a mannered hand in protest, bowed slightly and murmured, "If it is your pleasure."

Of course the cocktail came with a cherry. I had resigned myself to it, and was determined there must be nothing to cloud the elegant aura of our celebration. I spoke not a word.

But Priscilla would have none of it. With a few imperious gestures she brought back our starched friend, and pointed accusingly toward the cherry, quoting me verbatim.

The gentleman's face assumed an expression about halfway between a tolerant smile one would bestow upon children or inmates of a mental institution, and an outright sneer. Picking up my drink, he reached in with his manicured fingers, extracted the cherry, and popped it into his mouth. Then he replaced the cocktail before me, turned around and departed.

Again, I didn't want to spoil our evening. But *he* had, for we steamed our way through the food, with sweet nothings and *bons mots* forgotten.

To this day I have not determined what we *should* have done. I alternate from physical violence to meek acceptance. I chose the latter, perhaps because physical violence is not something I do well.

A while ago I joined a dinner party at Yamashiro's, a charming Japanese restaurant high in the hills overlooking the twinkling lights of Hollywood below. The attractive Japanese waitress bobbed a polite greeting and spoke:

"You like cocktail?"

"Yes," I said. And I recited my litany about a Manhattan cocktail without a cherry.

She disappeared, and a moment later returned. "Sir," she said, obviously embarrassed, "we have no cherries."

My fellow guests looked startled. But of course they lacked my background of traveling in the orient.

"Do you have olives?" I asked.

She nodded happily. "Oh yes, sir."

"Then bring me a Manhattan without an olive," I said calmly. And she did.

Regarding my Manhattan problem, I have long since withdrawn from the lists, but strangely enough Priscilla caught up the falling lance and now couches it bravely. She orders a vodka sour with an egg white, which involves separating the white of an egg, and whipping it in a blender, along with other ingredients. (I always wonder what happens to the yoke.) Amazingly, she seems to get this brew, properly and courteously served, even in the lowliest bistro. I am sure she enjoys the drama of the situation rather than the basic booze. And it does seem to prove that it's easier to get something *added* than something *removed*. There's undoubtedly a fine moral to be extracted from that statement but I haven't been able to find it.

* * *

I'm sure you've heard the old cliché defining repartee as "What you think of on the way home." Normally glib enough, there have been occasions in my variegated career when I have been unable to come up with a proper rejoinder, and have departed nourishing a feeling of profound inadequacy. The cherry episode was of course a memorable one. But then there was another, long ago, that still bugs me.

I was enjoying myself at a club in Manhattan called the Place Elegante. It was in an old brownstone building, known perhaps only to habitues, for if there was any sign on the outside, I never noticed it. The building was said to have once belonged to a branch of the Woolworth family, and there is some lurid tale told of a murder or suicide with the body tumbling down the handsome staircase leaving a trail of blood on the carpet. I liked the place. It had a homey atmosphere, with a magnificent bar, good food, and — most important to me — a very fine gentleman who played the piano. I remember him only as "Bill."

It was the custom of guests, in a festive mood, to cluster around the piano. Bill would play their requests, especially college songs, which would be bellowed by all attending grads.

I had not attended college, but knew all the songs, and could hold my own vocally with most, and enjoy the good fellowship.

One night I was there with a few chaps from the office, who insisted on continuing their business discussion at the dinner table. Bored, I wandered over to the piano and joined the group in an emotionally charged version of "The Whiffenpoof Song."

As other softer and sweeter songs followed, I became aware of a charming young lady beside me. It wasn't her cute face and absolutely devastating figure and décolleté that interested me, but her voice. I inquired if she had studied for the opera. She said no, she just liked to sing.

She also liked to drink. I ordered another martini for her as Bill started "The Sweetheart of Sigma Chi." Our rendition was truly outstanding. Clutched in each other's arms, cheeks touching, we reached the final phrases in such ringing harmony that the other contestants drew back, applauded and shouted loud huzzas.

Unfortunately, our routine attracted a certain amount of interest on the part of surrounding diners. For a large and visibly muscular chap rose, stepped over, and extended his hand to me in an obvious gesture of congratulation. The warmth of his greeting was a bit painful. He *squeezed*. I was beginning to wonder if I would ever play the banjo again, when he let go, and leaned forward, towering over my six feet as he hissed, "Do you think I'm cute, too?"

The young lady's expression suggested definitely that she was the girl he brung. She looked alarmed and beat a hasty retreat to the ladies' room. Unfortunately, I could not follow.

To this date I have not come up with a suitable response for "Do you think I'm cute, too?" Had I said "Yes" he would have surely found the inference offensive. A negative reply could have been interpreted as derogatory. Any position in between, such as "Oh, I don't know . . . I've seen better" might have earned for me a place in immortality with the Woolworth heir.

The only thing I am sure of is that it dampened my joie de vivre for the evening. I joined the business discussion back at my table.

20

The mighty blast of a ship's whistle brings to many people a nostalgic urge to be aboard at that magic moment . . . when everyday ties are cast off with the ship's hawsers and we sail majestically down the harbor, out to sea.

To me, that shattering sound produces a flush of embarrassment. For it brings to mind an episode in which the leading role was played by a clown. Me.

I had crossed the Atlantic many times by plane. It offered advantages, businesswise, because it placed your body in London a relatively few hours after leaving Los Angeles. A major disadvantage to me was that my mind did not arrive at the same time. Due to the drastic time change I would sometimes sit zombie-like at an early meeting, while vital affairs were discussed. A day or two later, I would be screaming indignantly about decisions I had approved yesterday . . . or so they told me.

The simple mathematics are that when you leave Los Angeles at noon, you arrive in Europe at 11:00 P.M., ready for a hot bath and a good night's sleep. Only it's six or seven in the morning with everybody bright-eyed, eager and ready to have at you.

At least that was the story I told my boss, Glenn Wallichs. His response was something to the effect that "We get back at them when they come over here," which I considered cavalier. I told him I had a better solution.

The idea was I would take a ship from New York to Southhampton. The *United States* left at noon Thursday and arrived very early on Tuesday morning, where I would step ashore, rested, well-briefed — for I would have had many quiet hours to pursue pertinent reports — and ready to stand toe-to-toe with Britain's Finest. QED.

But Wallichs had funny ideas. I gathered that there was something immoral about taking a ship. He somehow visualized me leaning against bars, leering at lady passengers, and wasting my energies on the dance floor.

It was a challenge to my integrity that I could not ignore. Shortly thereafter, I found myself on the spacious deck of the *United States*, waving joyously at a group of old friends standing on the drab pier as the ship moved away. It's a wonderful feeling.

I don't mean that I was glad to leave these friends behind. Because they had appeared en masse, carrying a fine assortment of bottled goods, and for the past two hours we had been toasting happy memories of yesteryear, and gyrating to the marvelous ship's orchestra, led by the well-known Meyer Davis. In fact, I remember telling him of the band's great recording potential if he would pick up the tempo a bit, at which point he handed me the baton. The orchestra responded capably to my vigorous beat, and everyone agreed that the improvement was most gratifying.

It was high noon when we sailed out of the harbor. As a New Yorker I had seen the Statue of Liberty, so I retired to my cabin for a brief siesta before tea time on deck. I had one of the few single rooms available. It was on the uppermost deck, wedged in between the kiddies' playroom and assorted deck activities, like shuffleboard. Towering above me was the monstrous stack, supporting the ship's whistle. (There should be a better word than "whistle" for that shattering sound-producer, but I can't find any!)

I was suddenly awakened by the loudest blast that had ever assailed my eardrums. The room actually vibrated under it. And then again! I could hear running feet, and voices. Trouble!

It took a moment for me to realize where I was. Then I leaped to my feet, pulled on my pants, stepped into shoes, and dashed down the stairs to the promenade deck below, as I slipped on a jacket.

It was quite obvious that the situation was serious. For all passengers and crew members wore bright orange life preservers.

Then a loud voice came over the public address system. An irritated voice.

"Will the gentleman in the blue jacket either put on a life preserver for the drill or return to his cabin until it is over!"

I looked at my sleeve. It was blue. I looked up at my fellow passengers. They were glaring at me. I slunk back up the stairs. My debut on shipboard, and I had flubbed it. Humiliating.

But I was not to be caught a second time! Following a night that gave me an excellent chance to become acquainted with a great many passengers, my blissful sleep was again interrupted by the mighty blast from the overhead funnel. In an instant I was out of bed, strapping on my lifebelt and galloping down to the promenade deck.

160

But it was strangely peaceful ... passengers lolling on deck chairs, munching on little cakes, relaxed.

And there I stood in my flaming orange belt. They looked at me with curious amusement. Some kind of a nut, no doubt. It seems the whistle had merely announced the noon hour, a daily procedure. Again, I slunk back to my cabin.

*   *   *

On a later date, I made the same crossing on the beautiful new French liner named *The France*, for the country of its origin, no doubt. Remembering the *United States* as a U.S. ship, I envied the simplicity of name selection for such craft. For I own a small sailboat, and the difficulty of selecting an appropriate name was something I would like to forget.

The boat, for you who are knowledgeable, is a Cal-25. I bought it "used" from a youngish swinger who had found it convenient for floating assignations. He called it *"Sockittome,"* a name I found incompatible with my age, dignity, and marital status. Having removed the name from the boat, and assorted bottles from cupboards below decks, the question was what to call it.

Many boats are named after wives and/or sweethearts. Priscilla didn't like *"Priscilla"* — she said it was too long. A friend came up with *"Miss Pris,"* which I thought rather catchy but she termed too "prissy."

One cannot arbitrarily name a boat "Gwendolyn" or "Gladys" without some derivation. Priscilla took a dim view of my calling the boat "Helen" after a former girl friend of whom I had been very fond. I switched to things like "Sea Fever," but discovered we already had two at the yacht club and many more, no doubt in the marina. Priscilla, who found my prowess as a sailor lacking, suggested *"Chicken of the Sea,"* which was not as clever as she seemed to find it.

I wound up calling it *"Boojum,"* over her objections. She said nobody would know what it meant. This may be true among the "illiterati" but, as you no doubt know, it is from Lewis Carroll's *The Hunting of the Snark*.

The story tells of a strange crew of assorted people and animals putting out to sea on a search for a Snark. When far out on the ocean it is discovered that no one is quite sure of what a snark *is*. But one chap — the carpenter, I believe — states that he *does* know that when you find the snark — and it turns out to be a boojum — you would forthwith vanish away ... or words to that effect. I thought *Boojum* had a quaint, literary flavor, and enjoyed the aura of superiority it gave me over friends who'd say things like "What in hell is a boojum?" Then I'd pour another drink, relax, and say, "You mean to tell me that you — a Ph.D. from Stanford — never heard of etc. and etc." Rather pleasant.

But Gene Frost, a friend and neighbor, sent me a note recently stating, "I'll bet you didn't know that all the time you were naming your boat after a cactus." Enclosed was an article entitled "A Boojum Blossoms in Baja." Seems it is a rather inferior and unattractive species of desert cactus that grows only a half inch a year. The article states the name was given the plant by Godfrey Sykes, a botanist exploring Sonora in 1922. He looked at the scaly stems intently with the aid of a microscope and said, "Ho, ho, a boojum — definitely a boojum!". . . . Or so his son Alberton relates. Mr. Sykes was obviously well read. You might like to know that a Dr. Robert R. Humphrey, a University of Arizona professor emeritus, is completing a book on the findings of five years' research on the boojum's ecology. The article states "The book will be the only comprehensive work of its kind to date." No doubt.

* * *

But back to the huge and gracious *France*. It had sleek lines, high-style decor, and a cuisine that defies description. We had two elaborate suites . . . an extravagance perhaps justified because our entourage included Priscilla, her mother, Mrs. Paul A. White, her sister, the glamorous actress Patricia Barry, and the grand old actor Bill Frawley, who is best remembered as "Fred" in "I Love Lucy." Bill looked Irish and was. Yet he had never been to Ireland. So Patricia, who had acted with him on many occasions, invited him to join us, and we included Dublin on our itinerary. He had a sharp wit, and we all traded quips with enthusiasm.

The most important area of the *France* is not the bridge, where the boat is navigated. And the most important person is definitely not the captain. It's the beauty parlor, and the hairdresser. The ladies in our group had been well briefed and appointments had been made for the entire trip before we left port . . . coinciding with the various social functions. Women with a more naive or casual attitude, who ambled in for a hairdo hours after sailing were confronted by solid bookings and spent a good part of the trip panting after cancellations.

All this was understandable, when one experiences the first dinner on the *France*. It's the second sitting, of course — only rustics and children attend the first. And we *never* arrived at the designated time. Because there was a large and beautiful staircase, that curved its way into the dining area below. Ladies arrived at the top, gorgeously gowned and groomed. After pausing a few dramatic moments, while all eyes paid homage, they undulated down the steps to their tables, smiling with tolerant charm at their stumbling escorts who had been boozing it up in the lounge while waiting for the curtain to rise on the production.

Our group had somewhat of an edge over most, because we had some real pros in it, headed by Patricia, who could make an entrance into a hardware store dramatic. Bill Frawley, while no Don Juan, was well known and beloved, and always had a happy glow to his face, aided by the Long Wait for the Ladies, and Dunn's good company on the next barstool. Priscilla could hold her own, because of her natural beauty, good figure and three hours of burnishing it all. And Mrs. White lent dignity and distinction, as she descended the stairs, supported on Bill's arm. (She insisted it was the other way around, because she was constantly anticipating his wavering footsteps missing a foothold, and tumbling down like Humpty Dumpty.)

I had decided to play my own role as halfway between Rock Hudson and John Wayne . . . gay, carefree, but with inherent dignity. Fortunately I had purchased new evening clothes for the production. My old tux dated back to my orchestra days, and even casual examination could reveal a roundish worn area on the jacket, where my banjo rested, rubbing away as I thumped it. No doubt, many people were saying, "But who is *he*?" I left the question unanswered, basking in the reflected glory of the group.

It was quite a trip, dampened only when we reached Dublin. Bill Frawley didn't like the country or the Irish. We were all charmed by the place, but he snorted his disenchantment, due, I am sure, to his advanced years and missing the familiar comforts of home.

As for me, I found the Irish in Dublin and thereabouts gentle, kind and delightful people. In New York, I remembered them as colorful and capable, but alarmingly pugnacious. On more than one occasion I have hesitated to mention that my heritage was Welsh, not Irish. Irishmen with my name usually spell it with an "e" dangling at the end. I have also neglected to emphasize the family's Protestant affiliation, for I was not by nature a troublemaker.

Bill didn't like England either, and he left ahead of schedule for home. I missed him, because he was a lot of fun to be with, especially during the short eternities when we were waiting in the bar for the ladies to appear. He died not long afterwards, collapsing on Hollywood Boulevard after attending a movie theater . . . perhaps as good a way as any for him to leave us.

* * *

I must say a word more about Priscilla's sister, who became Patricia Barry when she married Philip Barry, son of the famous playwright. Tish, as we called her, possessed striking beauty, and ruled her dominion of admirers with the traditional "whim of iron." At one time the entourage included Howard Hughes, who thrilled Priscilla with a floral offering at the birth of our second son. But we never met him, for he operated then, as now, in a haze of obscurity. A strange man. Surely enough has been said about him, with my alma mater McGraw-Hill paying too much for the privilege, but I must recall the days when I first saw him. . . .

We were shooting a serial at the old Metropolitan Studios in Hollywood, and shared it with but one other company who were making

"Hell's Angels." The gangling, youthful Hughes, ambling about in knickers, first hired a director but quickly fired him and took over. The picture was started with Greta Nissen, a beautiful Scandinavian actress, in the lead. But along came talkies, and her accent did not fit the role of an English girl. Perhaps it could have been dubbed, but not with Howard Hughes around. He reshot a good deal of the picture, again building the vast ballroom of Buckingham Palace, which had been dismantled after earlier shooting.

And, of course, he brought in Jean Harlow. We used to sneak away from our sets to leer at her through the wings. In fact she was developing the voyeuristic potential of our entire company when came the sad day that the set was marked "Closed to Outsiders."

But he treated his crew well. It was management's custom in our company to take everybody off salary the minute the camera crank stopped turning. Hughes kept them on ... perhaps because he might decide to reshoot the picture with a new protégé. Whatever the reason, his staff loved it and we envied them.

Right after the war, houses were almost impossible to rent, particularly those that would accept children. So we shared a house with Patricia. The house had a thatched roof, moss for a lawn, and was referred to as the "Gnome Home." It worked out fine except that constant foot traffic and phone ringing had a tendency to shake our family's domestic tranquility. For every phone message was of vital importance to Tish and every visitor significant to her career.

I remember one evening I was reclining in the only comfortable chair the house contained, reading a complex business report, while I sipped a highball. Real peaceful, like the way I'd hoped married life would be.

Then, of course, the phone rang. And simultaneously the front door opened and a large gentleman I had never seen before burst in and snatched up the phone. He seemed puzzled and annoyed, ultimately slamming down the receiver.

"It wasn't for me," he snapped. I somehow got the feeling it was my fault, and murmured apologetic noises, as Tish came down to greet him.

But all in all, we were delighted to have the house and yard at that time, and I even got adjusted to the general attitude that we were poor relatives, enjoying a movie star's largesse.

21

"Where are *you* folks going on New Year's Eve?"

Our friends always ask this question with an air of jovial anticipation. And you can bet it is asked because they want to tell you where *they* are going. And what *she's* going to wear.

Only a social leper would reply, "Well the fact is that Lloyd and I weren't invited anywhere. So we're planning to stay home and stare at each other through dinner, then catch an old movie on television — Lloyd is crazy about Claudette Colbert. He loves that hitchhiking scene where she pulls her skirt up to her knee. Then he goes to bed at ten thirty, so when midnight comes I'll raise a glass of buttermilk and kiss Harvey." (Harvey sleeps during the day. He's our cat.)

Priscilla has actually made a remark like that. I know, because I heard her. Of course I recognized it immediately as an age-old stratagem designed to humiliate me into some sort of rash action like getting reservations at the Whoopdedo Club where drinks, funny hats and favors, and a late supper are available for an amount sufficient to finance Jon's freshman year at college — if one includes the new dress Priscilla always must have, so I won't be ashamed of her.

You will all hate me for this but I'm going to say it. I find a New Year's Eve party a *Big Fat Bore.*

It never lives up to its billing. It *couldn't.* Because the kind of orgy anticipated for that super-special night just isn't going to evolve, among a bunch of friends, or worse, relatives, who know too much about each other. The very *obligation* to go leaping about and screaming funny remarks as the magic moment approaches, places too great a strain on one's credulity, not to mention things like fallen arches.

At least that's my attitude. And I can hear Priscilla saying, "Now that you've opened your big mouth about it in print, we'll never be invited *anywhere* again!" So I hasten to add that we *are* available the other 364 evenings, and a jolly couple we can be.

I think my abhorrence was born in the days long ago when I played in dance orchestras. New Year's Eve was our chance for the Big Killing. For along with the maitre d', captains and waiters, we clipped the public with rapacious enthusiasm.

I would sit on the stand, beating my banjo and gazing at the actions of adolescent oldsters with a hauteur that only a very young man can generate when watching such folks enjoy themselves.

And when, by the dawn's early light, I took my share of salary, overtime and tips, I wondered why grown-up people paid so much for so little. I still wonder.

All this leads me to a New Year's Eve that I spent on a deluxe train. Our company was having a big sales meeting in New Orleans on January 3rd. Alan Livingston, Hal Cook and I discovered we mutually hated New Year's Eve and we decided to take the train that night, leaving at about seven. The more we talked about it the more enthusiastic we got. Surely there'd be a real swinging crowd aboard and we'd have a ball. We got to talking to our colleagues about it, and soon became the envy of those who were trapped in town that night and would fly out in routine fashion just before the meeting.

So on the last night of the year we kissed our morose wives farewell and boarded the Santa Fe Chief for fun, fun, fun.

The train pulled out as I was getting settled in my stateroom . . . we moved on through the industrial area and ultimately the orange groves and over country beyond. It was pleasant and peaceful.

We had agreed to rendezvous at eight in the club car, so after careful grooming I opened my door and stepped out to embrace my opportunities. As I walked through the cars, heading toward the back of the train, I began to feel vaguely uneasy. They were completely empty. Perhaps the railroad was planning to drop them off at Yuma or somewhere.

Alan and Hal were in the club car ahead of me. I looked at them and spoke the classical line, repeated through the centuries by men-on-the-prowl: "Where's the action?"

"Over there," Alan said, pointing down the aisle. She was a sweet little old lady of the sherry-sipping type. She probably got on at Pasadena and, in deference to the occasion, had changed her tennis shoes to patent leather pumps.

It seems we were the *only* passengers on the entire train!

Having nothing better to do, we consumed endless cocktails, toasting our friends, our future, our pasts, and lots of other things.

Then we started framing a story for the boys at the meeting who would want every lascivious detail about the "living ball" we had had on the train.

As the drinks and miles were consumed the script improved. We worked on it during the entire trip. There was nothing else to work on.

As we neared our destination, the story had blossomed into a near-nude orgy. Seems we had shared the train with a group of models and show girls who were on their way to participate in Mardi Gras parties. The story got so real we began looking around the train for them.

Amazingly, the boys at the meeting believed us. In fairness, I think I should get most of the credit, because I threw in little succulent details, with sly sniggerings, that highlighted each Big Fat Lie with a purple patina. Our trip was a great success, we all agreed. The only problem was back-pedaling to the truth when we returned home to our wives.

* * *

My first train trip was as a very young man, when I left Brooklyn to join my brother, Lin, in Hollywood. He was an assistant cameraman and had wangled a job for me as a reader in the story department of Pathé-DeMille. I was in my early twenties and thrilled at the opportunity.

My mother, wonderful woman that she was, maintained her composure as her second and last son left. In those days, before plane travel, people didn't jet around, and particularly in our orbit where money was hard to come by. It would be at least a few years before she would see me again, that was sure. I was sitting by the open car window as the "All aboard" sounded. I could see she was fighting to control her grief and I kept chattering away about coming back soon, writing often. . . .

Then the train started and slowly gained speed. She kept step with it for a moment or two, then stopped, as the tears that she could no longer control came.

Forgive me if now, so many years later, I pause to pay loving tribute to the memory of a woman whose character, talents, courage, and self-sacrifice held our family together through long periods of desperate need and personal pressures. It's a long story that has no place here, but to this day my brother and I cannot discuss it without deep emotion. She gave so much of herself and got so little in return.

My seat partner on the train turned out to be an elderly farmer. He kept pointing out crops to me as we rolled across the country on our five-day trip to the West Coast. Conversation was difficult for me because as a born-and-bred New Yorker, I had seldom seen a horse that didn't have a policeman on it, and our vegetables were all store-bought. But I did try my best to appear interested, because he was such a nice old gentleman.

What I couldn't understand was why he never went into the dining car. My brother had sent me money for the ticket and meals. But when I suggested to my seat partner that he join me in the dining car, he always said, "Thank you — not now."

Then late one night I discovered what it was all about. I was tossing around in my upper berth when I heard, above the click-clack of the rails, a noise . . . a crunch-crunching. For a moment it reminded me of when I lived in Florida, as a boy, and slept on a cot in the attic. Every night termites were apparently munching away on the beams overhead . . . because next morning the covers were full of sawdust and I had to brush it out of my hair.

This crunch, I finally figured out: the old gentleman was eating soda crackers. He had a five-day supply to cover the trip, and about midnight he'd consume his daily "meal." He admitted later that he could barely scrape together enough money for his train fare, so he ate crackers in his berth, because he was embarrassed to do so before his fellow passengers.

There is nothing especially significant about this incident, but somehow I've never forgotten it. Particularly his discomfort when I tried to invite him to the dining car as my guest. I know I shouldn't have done it, and yet felt I must. When we arrived in Los Angeles I was happy to see him greeted warmly by a young woman, perhaps his daughter. I hope she was a good cook.

* * *

A memorable train was the one that went from New York to Philadelphia. During the war, businessmen took it when they couldn't get hotel rooms. Pennsy had a sleeper train that left about midnight, and after the two-hour ride to Philly, pulled off on a siding, where the passengers could sleep until morning, when it went back to New York, serving a nice breakfast en route.

That sleeper has long since passed into history. But not so long ago, I took the train from New York, planning to have dinner on it and arrive in Philadelphia about seven thirty. Philadelphia was, and probably still is, a "tryout" town for shows in the pre-Broadway state. Night after night, author, producer, director, entrepreneur, and other assorted participants involved in a new show, would wrangle over bits of dialogue, action, and staging. Then the staff would sit up all night making changes, which would be rehearsed in the morning and incorporated in the show that evening — for better or worse. By the end of the tryout period, the whole group, especially the cast, were candidates for a mental institution. Then the show either died on the spot or headed for Broadway for that exquisite torture known as "opening night." Now they have preview performances, which seem to me only to prolong the torture.

A recent opening night that I am sure paid off was "Jesus Christ, Superstar." Everyone was requested to dress in "contemporary" evening clothes. The show was staged in Universal's new outdoor theater, and it was a cold night. Army blankets were offered for sale at ten dollars each, and a vigorous business was carried on among the shivering ladies, who had sought to out-nude each other, and wound up concealing their goodies under scratchy, drab blankets. The show didn't really need the support of this financial windfall, but, like popcorn at the movies, it all helps.

But this train to Philadelphia ... it was a sorry mess, when we boarded it to assess a new show in Philly. There had apparently been either no time for or no interest in cleaning it between trips. What a contrast to "the good old days." We decided to pass up the dining car, on the theory that it was under the same management. I had planned to take a late train back, after the show, but changed my plans in favor of a room at the hotel and flying back in the morning.

The production was Meredith Willson's new one, "The Unsinkable Molly Brown." Meredith had been a good friend since the days of "Music Man," a show which had been turned down by almost every major and minor producer, until Kermit Bloomgarten took it under his wing and it opened to become one of the greatest, and surely the most innovative, musicals of all time.

I thought "Molly" was a worthy successor. But Meredith was twitching with anxiety. You may recall that Molly, a girl of humble background, wanted most of all to have her very own brass bed when she married — a status symbol consistent with her grinding ambition. The man who yearned to make her his wife had built a home to entice her into his arms. And in the bedroom was the biggest and brightest brass bed you ever did see!

Meredith wanted to conceal the bed on stage, until, in a sweeping gesture, it was revealed, to the oh's and ah's of Molly — and the audience. But Dore Schary, the producer, approved a set that revealed the bed in the glaring spotlight the moment the curtain rose for the scene.

No surprise. No charm. No gasps of delight. While no one asked my opinion, I agreed with Meredith. Strange is "show biz," when talented people can disagree. Mr. Schary won, and I think the audience lost.

22

"Just what in hell *do* you like?"

This is a question I somehow feel I should answer, in view of the fact that I've spent a good many words in this book complaining about successful hotels, basically nice people, well-operated airlines. . . .

It is obvious, I am sure, that a writer never *gains* readers by filling pages with nice things about places and people. We all want to hear about the man who comes home from work two hours late and bashes his wife on the head because his martini isn't properly chilled. But who cares about the chap next door who stopped to pick up some flowers and kisses his wife tenderly, despite the horror of her crown of curlers and her warm greeting, "*You* already? I didn't realize it was so late."

No, this is not what lawyers call a "disclaimer." I still loathe the desk clerk at the Woodbury, the maitre d' who messed up my Manhattan, and a host of others. It gives me great pleasure to malign them in print. And I suspect most people would rather read about such creatures than about nice dull people like you and me, who go pottering about, doing appointed tasks as best we can, paying our taxes and supporting our families in a manner far exceeding our means.

But I am occasionally asked to recommend a hotel, or restaurant, or vacation spot. So perhaps I should say a positive word or two here . . . bearing in mind that tastes vary, and mine are perhaps jaded from years and endless miles of travel.

I remember once Leopold Stokowski came up to me at a cocktail party stating he'd heard I was a native New Yorker and wondered what restaurant I preferred above all others. My mother had always told me to speak the truth so I answered, "Chez Vito." He looked amazed as he said "Why?"

"Because it has a romantic atmosphere and a beautiful string group

171

who play selections from operettas," I said . . . remembering the years that noble bistro had offered such a romantic background for my dalliances.

The maestro snorted. "That's a stupid reason for picking a restaurant!" he growled and walked away. He was quite a gourmet, I am sure, but also not insensitive to other delectable nuances. I remember when he signed a contract with Capitol in my office. We had a photographer and a publicist present and he was supposed to sit at my desk, holding the pen and looking happy, while I stood at his shoulder, basking in the glory of it all.

But he wouldn't look at the contract. He was looking at Marilyn, my lovely blonde secretary who had big blue eyes and a curvaceous figure. "Marilyn *Monroe*?" he asked her archly, indicating his mind was not on his work. Marilyn, who knew every warped cranny of my mind, recognized my "Scram, kid!" look and departed.

All this explains, I trust, that I sometimes recommend things for peculiar and personal reasons, and you would do better to trust your travel agent, who has never been there and has no prejudices.

* * *

A few days ago I read a newspaper feature by Hal Burton, a notable book reviewer, called "Are the Classics All that Good?" I have never met Mr. Burton, but if I bump into him at a cocktail party someday, I hope I spill my Manhattan down his Countess Mara necktie. Any man who condemns Victor Hugo as a bore, stating, "What Hugo needed was a good editor to cut his copy to the bone . . ." and then praises lengthy, meandering Dickens, and God help us, the windiest of them all, Tolstoy's interminable *War and Peace* . . . please, Hal!

Hugo, master of plot construction and vigorous narration; Tolstoy great in concept, and in his sensitivity to humanity . . . but how I fought my way through those endless pages, trying to keep track of the host of characters . . . just to reach that magic moment when I could hold up my head among my peers and say casually, "*War and Peace*? Of course I've read it."

Lest you think this treatise is evolving into a literary critique, be it known that I have a point to make, related to my general theme. Mr. Burton has every right to his opinion, particularly as he is paid to express it.

I, who am reasonably well read but certainly not erudite, still can disagree vehemently with him. Thus, when I recommend or condemn hotels, restaurants, and such, it might pay to recall that on occasion I have differed with the experts, brash fellow that I am.

What's the best hotel in the world? I'll tell you what my traveling colleagues say. It's the Century Plaza, right here in smoggy Los Angeles

. . . new, beautiful and well operated. I haven't stayed there because I'm expected to sleep at home when in town, or answer questions.

My personal laurel goes to the Peninsula in Kowloon, Hong Kong. It's not glittering, like the Mandarin or the Hilton, but . . . well it seems to supply everything human needs require, attractively, quickly, and with maximum comfort. The service is incredible. You won't believe it but I have sat in my room and decided to send out soiled clothes for fast laundering. Before I could reach for the phone, my room boy would open the door and say, "May I take your laundry, sir?" Extrasensory perception must be part of his training.

I think New York has the edge on "worst hotels," with the runner up perhaps Paris. I can't get too specific — legal action is so costly these days. But the New York Hilton lobby has all the charm of Grand Central Terminal. And, as a friend of mine said about the Americana, "It's OK, but too far from the beach."

The Plaza should be superb with its Old World décor, and beautiful location. It isn't. I like the Essex and Hampshire Houses. And some of the small hotels are excellent, but lack adequate facilities for businessmen.

In Paris, I've stayed at the Prince de Gualle, Georges Cinq, Rafael, Grand, and a few others. It would be presumptuous of me to condemn so many establishments, so let me merely say that for various reasons I lack enthusiasm. Perhaps their lavishness did not blend with my Brooklyn background.

I'm happiest at a small but elegant Parisian hotel — the Lancaster. The management always remembers you, and greets the cab when you arrive. The rooms haven't been redecorated since the days of Toulouse-Lautrec. They're charming — not heavy and hung with velvet like the Plaza Athené, but "Frenchy" like a scene from "Gigi."

* * *

Of course language barriers add confusion to hotel service abroad. While English is usually spoken, it is not necessarily understood by the parties involved. For example, the word *benjo*, pronounced "banjo," means toilet in Japanese. Thus when I once mentioned that I played the banjo, being polite people they didn't question me. But I am sure they wondered how and why.

I remember the time I was in Beirut's impressive Phoenician Hotel with Priscilla. We were unable to enjoy our spacious room overlooking the sea, because both of us were in bed with some form of local dysentery that was really a grabber. I had phoned for the hotel doctor, for a quick cure was vital if we were to continue on our journey.

Instead, a nurse appeared. She was quite huge, with black hair, black eyes, bushy black eyebrows and a large black bag. Apparently our ailment was routine, for she flipped open the bag and approached me with a huge hypodermic needle that I always thought was reserved for horses. I shrank back in alarm.

"Show me your sex," she said.

Later Priscilla said I should have replied, "If I do, you will be disappointed." I personally favored, "I will if you'll show me yours." But of course I knew she wanted to plunge the needle into my buttocks, and I reluctantly exposed enough acreage to supply an adequate target. Priscilla was next, and in a short time we were on our feet, feeling better, and preparing to leave for Athens.

That particular leg of our trip was on Near-East Air Lines, run by an Arab group. I was a bit wary of it, but it was the only flight that day, and the eternal feud with the Jews was for the moment quiet. I must confess that the flight was delightful; the food was superb and the attendants charmingly helpful.

I recall an earlier trip on Pan Am, from Beirut to Athens. When the American stewardess asked me what I wanted to drink, I said, "A nice big cold glass of water — with ice!" For when you spend much time in strange countries you get tired of drinking beer and washing your teeth in warm Coca-Cola.

After I had drained the glass and was chomping on a fragment of ice cube, a thought crossed my mind. This was Flight 1, Pan Am's plane that goes hippity-hopping around the world every day.

"Where did you get this water?" I asked.

"Beirut," she replied.

* * *

Actually, the only place I am dead-certain-sure to have at least a touch of dysentery is in Mexico. Included in my duties was supervising Capitol's companies in Toronto, Canada, and Mexico City. As these cities were on the points of an equilateral triangle with Los Angeles, I flew them frequently, and always brought along a good long paperback for my stay in Mexico. (It gets dull, just sitting there.) One time I went from Toronto directly to South America. When we passed over Mexico City at 30,000 feet, I felt rumblings below the belt. It shows you how strong that bug is. I mentioned it to our Mexican partner, Victor Rivero, and he replied sympathetically, "I know — I have the same problem when I visit the States."

* * *

I must take a moment at this juncture to state that from the wealthiest social and business leaders, down to the humblest peons, I have found the Mexicans delightful, charming people. A major contact for me was Emilio Ascaraga, a youthful member of a well-known family who owned and operated most of the television and radio stations in the country. I was negotiating a 50-50 partnership with our company and the Ascaragas for a recording business in Mexico. And on this particular trip I carried a lengthy contract drawn up by our legal department in Hollywood, and covering, I am sure, every contingency known to the judicial mind.

I found Emilio waiting for me in the bar of the Maria Isabella Hotel. After greetings and a welcoming drink, I dropped the contract in his lap, with a dull thud.

"Emilio," I said, "my apologies for the size of this contract. I got it from our legal department. You give it to yours, and then we'll discuss it. No hurry, I know it's complicated."

Emilio weighed the tome in his two hands. Then he flipped to the rear pages, pulled out his pen, and signed with a flourish. With white teeth shining, he tossed it back at me.

Had *I* engaged in such a gesture our legal inquisitors would have been heating up the irons and oiling the rack, awaiting my return. But I like to think, first, that Emilio trusted me, and believed that what we had agreed to was in the contract — no more, no less. Perhaps, too, he felt that in any legal hassle, he stood little chance of losing in his native country. He was an important and powerful man in Mexico. And, I hasten to add, a good partner.

* * *

Bill Tallant, who was a sales executive for Capitol, tells a pleasant story about Mexicans at the other end of the spectrum. He was driving an old car to Acapulco, and wandered off on a side road to a small town. Here the car gasped, shuddered, and died.

A local garage man held an inquest, surrounded by a group of interested citizens. It was serious. Major surgery was essential. It would take three days.

Bill is a philosophical chap and he faced adversity with a brave smile. The garage man helped him to obtain lodgings. Then Bill asked where the telephone was. They had none.

"No *phones*?" Bill said, incredulously.

"No, señor," he explained. "Telephones bring *trouble*."

The more Bill thought about it the more he felt their point of view was not without merit. After several days of lolling about and getting acquainted, he was *sure* they had a point. Never had he felt more relaxed.

When the car was ready, and the moment of departure arrived, a large group of the townsfolk turned out. Pledges of eternal friendship were exchanged. Loud cheers echoed as Bill drove off, headed for the travail of civilization.

* * *

Toronto, another point on my triangle trip, was a sharp contrast to Mexico. Things were orderly, profitable and predictable . . . pleasant when you're responsible for the company, but not as much fun or challenge as Discos Capitol de Mexico.

I recall when we built a rather handsome complex of executive offices and warehouses near the airport. I was there for the gala opening for employees and their families. Our special guest was Sir Joseph Lockwood, head of all EMI's vast holdings and a prominent public figure in England. I had seen a good deal of him and he was at times explosive, but always stimulating.

As I entered our glittering new Canadian offices with Sir Joseph, I began to fear his reproof at our extravagance. Business facilities are a bit more spartan in the United Kingdom, and I wondered what was going through Sir J's mind as he eyed the employees, dressed in their Sunday best . . . men at the bar, and girls chattering happily, scattered about.

Sir Joseph looked at the scene with an expression I had seen on his face when reviewing the preliminary figures of an annual statement showing a decline in profits . . . or so it appeared to me. Then he spoke.

"Lloyd," he said, "I do believe the miniskirts here are shorter than in London."

I hadn't noticed, but later research proved him to be, as he usually is, absolutely right.

* * *

The subject of miniskirts causes my grasshopper mind to flip back to the days of my youth, when I aspired to be a commercial artist. I worked in an art studio, where I erased pencil lines from finished drawings, put on paper overlays, and went out to fetch sandwiches and coffee on command. I was classified as an apprentice and, to justify my title and my weekly salary of seventeen dollars, I was occasionally given a minor art assignment for a minor client who was behind on his payments. I always knew when this happy moment was about to arrive because one of the senior artists would imperiously shout, "Throw this bone to Lloyd."

But at seven o'clock, five nights a week, I doffed my Cinderella rags and donned regal robes. For that was the magic moment I attended art school, and stood before a large sheet of white paper, brandishing my charcoal like a professional. We all wore smocks, most of which were grubby and stained. Mine was quite new, but I aged it by slopping it with ink and rubbing charcoal into its coarse texture.

176

I was in a section of the school labeled "elementary," and for many a long winter evening, I came out of the snow, stood before my easel and made "cast drawings." The casts were plaster reproductions of the heads of Alexander the Great, Beethoven, and similar gentlemen of noble mien. We all did our best, with grim determination, for there are no dilettantes in night schools.

Then came that great occasion when I graduated to the life drawing class. I was a product of those pre-Playboy days when go-go girls were not twitching at your neighborhood beer parlor. Incredible as it may appear, I had never seen a live girl in the nude.

Now that moment was about to arrive. It was doubly exciting because I could stare at her with legitimate lechery.

I arrived early that night, selected an easel well up front, and was making a few practice parries in the air with my charcoal when the model arrived.

It was a nude model, sure enough. A large, hairy, muscular *man* wearing a bored look and a jock strap. I stared at him for two nights and concentrated on my work without distraction.

Then *she* arrived. A dainty, curvaceous miss, she slipped off her robe and stood under the spotlight, wearing absolutely nothing, while the instructor pointed out the obvious curves and emphasized the differences between this and our previous night's assignment. I tried to avoid staring at the pubic area, and assumed the casual, slightly bored look worn by older students. Much to my surprise I quickly gained control of my emotions and turned out a drawing that while not flattering, did bear some resemblance to the subject. In the process I discovered that nipples were not dead center on breasts, as depicted by Maxfield Parrish and Willy Pogoney, in their murals, but were off to the right and left. They were also not pointed . . . and I learned more about that aspect somewhat later in my career.

That night, after class, I took the subway back to Brooklyn with two other students. A young girl was seated directly opposite us, with a companion. Her skirt was short, and she had crossed her legs, exposing some very pleasant curves and a bit of bare thigh that disappeared into the shadows at a most critical area. We oggled, and nudged each other in lustful appreciation.

Then we got philosophical. Why were we so excited about *this* girl when we had just left a gorgeous and completely *naked* young lady . . . who instead of stimulating passionate thoughts, inspired us to smear charcoal about in a fairly creditable fashion? Why?

Then I think we found the answer. The thrill lay in *seeing something you weren't supposed to see*. In school, had we been engineering students, peering over the transom, it would have been highly stimulating. But standing in the room with the instructor emphasizing the curve of the buttocks, the situation was academic, we agreed.

177

Perhaps our present state of rampant pornography will be equally self-destructive. Eliminate the keyhole titillation and the mind need no longer supply those intriguing details not quite visible. Excluding such mental participation can change the wine of desire to purple Koolaid.

A theater showing pornographic movies on Hollywood Boulevard carries a sign stating, "Half Price for Senior Citizens." I suppose they only get half as much out of it. My office is right near the establishment. After passing it many times, I stopped at the box office.

"How do you define a senior citizen?" I asked the girl at the box office.

"You gotta have a Medicare Card," she said. I'm sure you'd need one, for I've heard it's rough on the prostate.

* * *

When Priscilla and I returned from a world tour, we were greeted by a neighbor who instead of inquiring about our enjoyment of Persepolis, said, "Will you help us fight the Sex Club?"

I learned, to my amazement, that this "club" had opened its doors almost directly across the street from us, slightly up the hill. It's a very fine residential neighborhood, with strict zoning, and with a full quota of children, from tots to teenagers.

Of all things, a doctor had leased out his home for this activity, and was reported to be an enthusiastic member. *Newsweek* ran a full page on the club, with vivid descriptions of its appointments. The features included a large room with a four-foot ceiling. On the floor, was a wall-to-wall water mattress. Participants somehow lubricated their bodies and were projected into the room from a chute, to join the happy, squirming group. For older folks, like me, there were small windows available for peering, and perhaps other more personal activities. Sounds sybaritic, and I can't vouch for it, but that's the story we were told by the irate neighbors who formed the vigilantes.

The sex club offered bus service for picking up clients, who left their cars in the parking lot of a distinguished and highly respectable bank, which rented it to them for off-peak occupancy. The driveway to the club entrance was protected by a ponderous wooden gate. When a button was pressed, it swung open and a large phallic symbol rose in greeting. Neighborhood children asked many questions . . . it seemed there must be some sort of Disneyland up there and they wanted to see it.

Strange how my friends reacted to this situation when I revealed it. They laughed and hooted and made all sorts of infuriating remarks and implications. I soon realized that as long as such a situation occurs in *somebody else's neighborhood*, it's funny! I'm waiting for my turn to laugh.

Getting rid of the club wasn't easy. Seems like legally it's no different from a bridge club or an ecology group. But it had violated building codes! So it was closed down, the gate was removed, and it now bears a "For Sale" sign. And the neighbors have gone back to fighting their crabgrass.

* * *

About the neighborhood . . . I want to expound a theory of mine that I feel represents a genuine breakthrough. It goes like this. . . .

Our houses are all somewhat large, and have spacious grounds and pools designed for enjoyment and relaxation. But when? Every time you start to "enjoy and relax" on your wrought-iron chaise with the flowered cushion, you stretch out your limbs and look around at all the goodies your labors have made possible.

But do you see these beauties of nature, and warm to the flashing sunlight as it glitters on the pool?

No! You note that weeds have become a creeping horror in your dichondra. And those expensive azaleas are not going to make it unless you start feeding and wheedling. And there are dozens of other nasty little observations that give you the nervous twitches.

Our house, for example, backs on the home of Efrem Zimbalist, the actor. A charming chap, he is, too. But he is raising one of the largest crops of bamboo in the state. It creeps over and under our fence, into our roses, the lawn and other areas, raising its nasty pointed head in endless array. It seems to grow almost a foot a day. I have heard that the Chinese, in early times, used to strap undesirable citizens over sprouting shoots, for a three-day impalement. In our place, the torture consists of watching it break through blacktop and lift concrete blocks in our patio. Come on over, and I'll show you what I suffer. My cries of pain brought over another neighbor, Max Mann, who returned with the construction crew used in his business who encircled the patio lawn in a steel jacket, sunk two feet deep. A kind act. But the bamboo will find a way around it, I am sure. It's what the nursery man calls "an aggressive feeder."

Now my plan is simply this.

Every weekend a group of compatible neighbors will *switch houses*.

I, for example, can lie supine in Gene Frost's patio chaise, basking in the beauties of his landscaping and glimmering pool, as I sip my highball. Gene has problems, I am sure, but if I do see them, which is unlikely, I will eye them with kindly tolerance, as I turn the pages of my paperback.

The Rosas, too, have a charming small house, somewhat neglected because he spends most of his time racing sailboats. But my eyes will pass over peeling paint with nary a shudder, for the problem is his, not mine.

Of course, some of my neighbors have a bit of eager-beaver in them, and will no doubt experience a compulsion to pluck weeds and trim dead branches at my house. If they do, I shall be under no obligation to reciprocate. The large flat of unplanted pansies at the Hackleys shall continue to grow, root-bound in their confinement, gaining barely a sympathetic glance from me. Life will be calm, peaceful and refreshing, with phone-answering limited by agreement to "They're not here."

Art Buchwald, my favorite columnist, recently came up with a similar plan, involving the exchange of teenage children. I can personally vouch for the soundness of his premise. Our son Jon, for example, when at home is laconic, nonsocial, and his dialogue at the dinner table is frequently limited to inquiries about extra helpings. Yet when on his own, in the homes of neighbors, we are told he is "utterly charming." We have asked for an explicit description to be sure we were talking about the same boy. We were. Other parents are equally astounded when we pour forth compliments about *their* offspring. It's all very confusing.

I am writing this on the day Jon left home for his freshman year at Rockford College, two thousand miles east of his home and parents. He kissed his mother, gently and with real affection. We shook hands, and I fought to resist embracing him, for he is a man now. He stood tall, tanned, husky and . . . yes, "utterly charming," I'm sure. Then he drove off.

Now Jeff, Jon, and Steve are all away at school. It's an experience many families go through but new to us. I will be most despondent, I know, on Wednesday nights, when the boys always put out the rubbish. Those cans are heavy.

23

Someone once said, "No man finds adventure unless he carries it with him in his soul."

I don't know what goes on in my soul, but I was usually able to return from a trip with a few new adventures packed in with my Rolaids and soiled laundry.

Mine, of course, were not the kind of experiences involving heroic deeds against incredible odds. They were garden-variety adventures . . . mild and middle-aged. If incredible odds loomed up, I ducked into a side street and ran.

But I was always able to take minor incidents and burnish them into intriguing affairs. Particularly when relating them later, at cocktail parties, after I returned from a trip and someone would say, "I suppose you found Singapore pretty dull without Priscilla along."

So I'd relate an experience. And there were occasionally those who would say, "Hey — y'oughta write a book." Normally, I am not susceptible to such flattery by my unlettered friends in their cups . . . having once said to a pretty girl with a plunging neckline, who painted pictures on weekends, "People pay lots of money for paintings not half as good!" She insisted on my buying one, then and there.

But I would enjoy, in my declining years, being singled out at parties as "He's the chap who wrote that book called . . . what *was* the title? Anyhow it was about . . . er . . . what in hell *was* it about, Martha?"

And Martha would say "He went to bed with a hooded cobra." Or, "He's that degenerate who's queer for Japanese massage girls." And I would smile graciously and try to be modest about the whole thing.

Because my career had an aura of excitement, I was recently invited to "The Adventurer's Club," in Los Angeles. Bill Berssen, Staff Commodore of the California Yacht Club, took me along, and I was curious to see what happened when a group with real qualifications got together.

The club facilities included a huge room where there were stuffed animals of every sort looking at us reproachfully through luminous glass eyes. The latest acquisition, which had just arrived, was a tremendous polar bear. The bear had been conquered in open combat by the donor, who told us he was an absolute sensation on the Hollywood Freeway as he hauled it in an open truck. He added, later, that his wife had made but one comment when he removed it from the house: *"Thank God!"* Some women have no pride in their husband's achievements. But I suppose building a décor around a polar bear presents difficulties.

It quickly became evident that all the club members had experienced a wide variety of *genuine* adventures — the kind I like to read about, in a comfortable chair before the fireplace, with a bourbon and soda close at hand.

A prospective member was introduced and asked to comment on his background. He was young and apologetic. All the poor chap had done was to parachute out of a plane into the midsummer heat of Death Valley, with a small survival kit tucked under one arm. Then he proceeded to hike several hundred miles to Las Vegas, in temperatures above 110°. I couldn't quite figure out *why* he did all this, because I hate going to Las Vegas even in air-conditioned planes. But he was well received and no doubt has a bright future.

I was afraid they'd ask me for a story, and I tried to think of one suitably impressive. The best I could come up with was being chased at 4:00 A.M., through a blizzard in a remote part of Vienna by a night club hostess because I wouldn't meet her demands for a hundred dollar tip. (No I *didn't* — I just *danced* with her!) I had no survival kit, but there was, fortunately, enough alcohol in my radiator to keep me from freezing. The story had some of the elements of battling a polar bear. (The hostess would have made an attractive display, stuffed.) But I was not called upon.

*　*　*

I made an honest effort to try to edit this book, to make it read smoothly. But I had to give it up. My manner of thinking and writing reminds me of an old correspondence school advertisement that must have been successful, for it ran many years. It showed a depressed, haggard-looking chap, sitting at his desk. Over his head were a dozen questions, oozing out of his mind, concerning changing his career, getting a different job, developing a new skill. In bold type the headline stated, "THE MAN WITH THE GRASSHOPPER MIND."

It reminds me of another famous ad . . . a similar chap at his desk. Only this time he is holding his head and looking dreadful. Seems like he has a bad hangover, but had to get to the office to keep his job. The

182

headline: "ON A MORNING LIKE THIS HIS FAILURE BEGAN." I used to think of that ad every time I woke up with a hangover, and I'd stay home to avoid being a failure.

I like music, art, writing, cocktails, girls, travel and many other things. I still do, though I've had to cut down here and there as the years pass. Looking for virtues, I can only think of one. I've never smoked. I can't think *why* I don't, because I've played in night clubs where the smoke was so thick I couldn't see the music, and it didn't bother me. One of the girls in the chorus used to blow smoke in my face when she sat on my lap backstage. I didn't mind it. Kitty Cassidy . . . my job included following her around the club. I accompanied her on the guitar as she'd sing one chorus of a song in front of each table and stand there until they tipped her. Sometimes we waited three or four minutes, silent and staring. I found the activity embarrassing. Kitty tried to give me half her tips but I wouldn't accept them, not wanting to be implicated in such a holdup.

My peculiar forte in that club was my ability to play songs no one in the orchestra knew — including me. Some drunk would come up, wave a bill in our faces and say, "D'ya know the Wassamahoozit Fight Song?" I'd always say "It's one of my *favorites* — you sing it and I'll play it!" Songs drunks request are harmonically similar and simple, so I'd fake along with him and finish with a loud flourish, joined by the band who had been creeping in as the melody line developed. We made lots of money that way, and these were tips I felt I earned.

* * *

Smoking always makes me think of Nat Cole. He was perhaps the greatest artist Capitol ever recorded. But more important, he was the finest gentleman I have ever known in all my years of recording work. Nat was pretty much of a chain smoker, and continued despite doctors' warnings. I was an honorary pallbearer at his funeral, surrounded by celebrities, silent in their grief. Someone said to Danny Thomas, "How did you get here, you were in New York last night?" His reply expressed how we all felt: "How could I *not* be here?"

I remember a bit of monologue Nat used in a show he produced. He was expressing the insecurity of life . . . "Where am I going? Where am I going to park when I get there?" I know, somewhere, there was a very special parking spot, marked with Nat Cole's name. And I'm sure it didn't take him long to start up a good harp combo. "And the Angels Swing" will be his first album.

* * *

If one has a moment of reflection before death closes in there must be no greater solace than knowing that you've been truly happy a good deal of the time . . . for surely this is what living is all about. Many people, sadly, do not *experience* happiness. They just *remember* it.

We had a neighbor who had every reason to be happy, yet she managed to extract utter misery out of such trifles as coffee spilled on a new carpet. When true tragedy touches her, she'll be reminiscing about the "good old days."

Having had more than enough sorrowful periods in my life, I have developed a ritual of regularly "counting my blessings." A corny cliché, maybe, but a good practice to retain one's perspective on the minor irritations that are a daily experience for most of us.

Are the Dunns happy? Yes, I am sure . . . despite Priscilla's ranting about a councilman's rape of our Santa Monica Mountains, and my recent operation in an area that is not available for public discussion. Our boys are all well and moving ahead. We have most of the goodies considered essential today, with enough money left over to support my sailboat and my bar bills at the California Yacht Club. And I believe I speak for Priscilla when I say we still get a kick out of being together . . . on most occasions.

When I was much younger, I used to collect definitions of happiness, perhaps because I knew so many unhappy people in New York. I personally felt the word was a bit too high-spirited and that "contentment" might be a fairer yardstick.

Wilson Wilmer, a good friend and fellow artist, once gave me a small book about the subject, declaring, "The happiest people are those who think the most interesting thoughts."

Nonsense. Was Schopenhauer happy? I've known some very happy dolts in my time. And who's to define what is interesting?

Another definition was "Happiness is doing what you like to do and getting paid for it." Not bad, though it eliminates all nongainfully employed.

Geishas, for example, seem very happy in their work. And let us understand clearly — it isn't what many foreigners assume. I just looked it up in the dictionary, to see how Mr. Webster would describe these ladies. He says, "A *geisha* is a Japanese girl who is trained to provide entertainment and light-hearted company, especially for men."

The lovely kimonos and graceful posturing are always pleasurable. But many geishas wear a stark white makeup of rice powder which I found pretty scary. I was told that there is one small area in the nape of the neck that is left unpowdered, and therefore *very sexy*. I have made several expeditions to check this out, but geishas' collars are high. I find it difficult to go casually peering down a girl's neck unless a décolletage is involved. In this area I have done considerable sly research perhaps because the objective, or objectives, seem more worth pursuing. It all shows how much custom and tradition affect one's libido.

I particularly recall one charming and gorgeously gowned and groomed geisha who was kneeling just behind me while I was eating.

Her mission was to serve me, and her proximity made me nervously conscious of my table manners.

I remember it so well. I was cautiously spooning some soup when a length of noodle got stuck on my lower lip and dangled unattractively. *Instantly* an exquisitely manicured hand glided past my ear and plucked the noodle from my lip with surgical finesse.

How charming! How much more gracious than the American way, when one's wife hisses, "You gotta noodle on your lip — quit gulping your soup!"

There are many other definitions of happiness, for many people are seeking to define and capture it. Maybe that's the trouble . . . like love or beauty, one cannot reduce it to words and phrases.

Neville Chamberlain, Great Britain's former Prime Minister, once reared back and gave this clinical analysis of happiness:

"The qualities that seem most conducive to happiness are steady nerves — ability to bear good fortune with moderation and bad fortune with constancy — insensitiveness to petty irritation — a sense of humor — a sense of balance and proportion — and an infinite capacity for doubting and questioning."

The author who quoted this, the American general Raymond E. Lee, adds that other desirable traits are "self-reliance . . . ability to profit intelligently by criticism without being unduly influenced by it, ability to concentrate on every problem by one's own reason and judgment, equally uninfluenced by the mob pressure of temporary majority opinion and the gilt and tinsel of rank and reputation."

Whew! Had enough? Then try this definition on for size. To me it encompasses almost all the vital elements. And it's easy to remember. It must be, for it is close to forty years since I first read it (I wish I remembered *where*, for I would like to give credit.)

Happiness comprises three ingredients:

1. Something to do.
2. Someone to love.
3. Something to anticipate.

Priscilla's life is constantly crowded with anticipation, because she is always getting involved in new things, like collecting assorted pink abominations called "Depression Glass," while taking courses in "Appreciation of Japanese Art" and "Mating Habits of the White Whale." She has tried on many occasions to shame me into joining her in such pursuits, and makes disparaging comments about my incipient senility when I decline to go with her.

Perhaps *you* can understand my attitude. For years my brain has been cluttered up with endless data about innumerable facts I needed in my work. Now that I have retired from an executive post with Capitol, I am trying to flush out of my mind things like the Gross National

Product of the Eleven Western States and the fact that noisy little girls from eight to thirteen represent a high percentage of today's record buyers. Such statistics depress me, and I am sure comprise the bulk of those little wrinkles in the brain you see in medical illustrations. I want to get my medulla oblongata nice and smooth, and then be a lot more selective about admitting new crevices.

One of my objectives is to try to avoid *argument* about *anything*. Impossible, of course, with war, politics, and a dozen other highly controversial subjects boiling away in daily headlines. And with so many stupid people around whose opinions differ from your own.

* * *

I have a constant conviction that today we are spending too much time and money hearing lectures and reading books that probe and analyze every human emotion. Sex comes to mind. (O.K. — so it usually does!) In my early youth I had only a vague concept of the physiology and psychology of it all. And it is with no attempt at double-entendre that I state that I learned the hard way. Each intriguing nuance — each tremulous discovery — embraced experiences that added to my understanding. I was Columbus, seeking a new shore . . . in contrast to today's tourist who has read all the guidebooks and seen all the pictures on television.

Young people of my station had no automobiles, with cosy seats. There were no shady byways for rendezvous in Brooklyn's noisy crowded streets. A colleague in my pursuit of happiness once sang, (with no apologies to Irving Berlin's "Always") our theme song: "I'll be loving you . . . in hallways."

Perhaps I was handicapped by dating what my mother referred to as "nice girls." There is nothing more jealously guarded than middle-class virtue. But it all sharpened my wits and techniques. One young lady exhibited, among other things, her erudition, as she quoted, "Thou hast all the arts of fine persuasion." That was the night I got my Ph.D.

Later, when a widower in my mid-thirties, I brought to the same charming pursuit a sophistication that eliminated a good bit of my early fumbling and frustration. But was it really more thrilling that way?

Thinking back I can find only one answer. It sure was!

* * *

"All too soon, life will end — in a calm gray blend," a poet wrote. Maybe his life was calm and gray. I can assure you mine is pleasantly pied. And I have a lot of things to look forward to. Anticipate.

For example, pop music seems to be moving from shattering sounds and unintelligible lyrics to something more melodic. And I can recognize the chord structure — even play a few of the new songs!

And young people are calming down, and adjusting their sights. My oldest boy, during his undergraduate years, insisted on majoring in classical music — the hell with his future security; do your own thing! Now he's a geologist, working for his Masters'. And specializing in stratigraphy — which, as you no doubt know, is the kind of speciality helpful in searching for oil. He's got it made.

I was in the barber shop the other day and two young men were lined up for haircuts. Their conversation indicated that they were trying to get summer jobs and wanted to make a good impression. "I *am* a troublemaker," one boy explained to me with a sly grin, "but I don't want to look like one!"

I read in the paper that black students are discovering that a stumbling knowledge of Swahili is of little help when seeking employment. They're switching to studying for vocations you can find in your local newspaper under "Help Wanted." I dare not comment further on this for fear of being misunderstood, but it all casts a hopeful glow on the horizon.

And, I must mention that I saw an album cover the other day that showed a large, luscious picture of a pretty girl, looking dreamily at a boy . . . only the back of his head showed, and his hair proved it was a man! (A reissue from earlier years? I hope not!)

Anyhow, suffused with a warm glow of gratitude, I was moved to pour a cocktail and raise my glass to whatever forces are ruling our destiny these days. Here's to *you*, out there! Cheers!

Then Priscilla came in and spoke:

"Isn't it awfully early in the afternoon to start drinking?"

* * *

Retired! Ah, the relaxation in not having to catch endless planes and go leaping around the world, as I did for so many years . . . putting out fires, starting others. And always decisions, decisions . . . with the hope that they were the right ones.

For despite the tone of levity in this book, I did spend a good deal of time in dull, grinding work, like most businessmen. And I had to be productive, because you can't charm your way out of a declining profit margin with bosses like Glenn Wallichs and EMI's Bill Stanford.

Mentioning Stanford reminds me that I got a letter from him the other day . . . speaking, as he says, "in the old personal atmosphere that pervaded over a cherryless Manhattan and a pink gin at 37,000 feet over the Pacific in a JAL DC 8 with a pretty Japanese hostess close at hand." He rambles on, and finishes:

"Well, Lloyd, I would like to hear again from you. I am becoming increasingly disenchanted with travel, but am off to South Africa again on the 1st of February. . . ."

Africa? Let's see ... TWA 840 leaves about noon and connects in Rome with South African Airlines — 3:05 P.M. for Johannesburg. Or Pan Am has a Paris connection with UTA. One could also go through Rio, and across ... or BOAC to London, and. ...

Hey, Bill — wait for me!

THE END